NOT WITH MY DAUGHTER!

A Dad's Guide to Screening Dates and Boyfriends

NOT WITH MY DAUGHTER!

TERRY VAUGHAN

Skyhorse Publishing

Skyhorse Publishing books may be purchased in bulk at special discounts for sales promotion, corporate gifts, fund-raising, or educational purposes. Special editions can also be created to specifications. For details, contact the Special Sales Department, Skyhorse Publishing, 307 West 36th Street, 11th Floor, New York, NY 10018 or info@skyhorsepublishing.com.

Visit our website at www.skyhorsepublishing.com.

10 9 8 7 6 5 4 3 2 1

Library of Congress Cataloging-in-Publication Data is available on file.

Cover design by Ashley Lau

Print ISBN: 978-1-62914-437-5
Ebook ISBN: 978-1-62914-915-8

Printed in the United States of America

CONTENTS

CHAPTER ONE
Reasons and Motivations

> "You have enemies? Good. That means you've stood up for something, sometime in your life!"
>
> —Winston Churchill

Once upon a time you might have described me as a "prepper." I had food, water, a selection of good knives, escape plans for virtually every contingency, and plenty of assorted firearms. In other words, everything a man would need in the event of a personal or global catastrophe. I was prepared for the world to implode. But as it turned out the Mayans only ran out of locations on which to write calendar dates beyond December 2012—they weren't predicting the world would end. That was our misinterpretation. They just ran out of walls to paint on.

So, in the absence of a natural or manmade disaster, I have come to realize that nothing is going to save me from my two daughters' coming of age, and yes, entrance into the dating scene. My older daughter is twelve, smart as a whip, athletic, and as feisty as me. She also believes the sun rises and sets with her dad, which is funny because she is the one I can most easily embarrass with a song or dance in front of her friends. With the teenage years on the horizon, I fear that her view of me being all-knowing is drawing to a close—at least temporarily. I'm hoping once she turns twenty-one those beliefs will return once again.

Then there is my middle child, my youngest daughter, who at age ten is already smarter than me. She could end up working for what's left of NASA, or even the CIA, because yes, she is *that* smart. Unfortunately, given her love of rock music and dancing, I'm afraid she might seriously consider being a Vegas showgirl. I console myself with the fact that if she does become a dancer it will be because of her love of music and not out of a sense of desperation to strike back at me. Contrary to Cora, Sophie isn't embarrassed by anything I do; she loves to laugh at me! So maybe I should be more concerned with Cora heading off to a life of glitz and glamour? She'd view the move as payback for all those times I goofed around in front of her friends. Parenting is tough, isn't it? And every single decision can have consequences—hell, even goofing off can come back to bite you on the ass!

With that being said, career choices are still a long way off, and I have more pressing concerns. Just like every other father in the world with daughters, I'm scared! I have been for years. I know it's my job and, of course, their mother's, to raise these girls and steer them clear of dangers along the way—and when I say "dangers," I mean little perverts commonly referred to as "teenage boys." How do I know that teenage boys are perverts? Hello, been there, done that. This is why I have no qualms about illuminating the pimply little buggers in such a nefarious light. I once walked in their shoes, and liked it. And that's what scares me the most!

Now I know I shouldn't be (unfairly) tarnishing every teenage boy with the same brush. There are certainly exceptions to the rule. For instance, my son will grow up as a gentleman and perfectly at ease around strong-minded women. He is already cognizant of how important it is to openly discuss his feelings, and he can thank his mother for that blessing. I, on the other hand, had to learn how to open up and share things like feelings under the patient tutelage of my wife. Years in the military coupled with my less-than-harmonious childhood worked together to make me the kind of guy who shut down emotionally when things became tough, or uncomfortable.

But today, I no longer think in terms of having to win everything, fix everything, or even have a well-thought-out response to a challenging question. I understand that none of those things matter as long as I am willing to talk, sometimes at great length, in a meaningful and caring way, and then listen to the response with all the attention it deserves! This is all going to be second nature to my son because if he doesn't listen, his momma takes offense and his sisters try to beat the crap out of him.

Now you may be a considerate, caring, well-adjusted, well-balanced, empathetic, and even sympathetic man who wouldn't hurt anyone—ever. If this is the case, then it's possible that your teenage experience was a wholesome one full of warm, fuzzy memories. You were most likely raised in a household with three square meals a day and a hug every night before bed, and there's nothing wrong with that. Hell, that's how we're bringing my son up. If one day my son (or a mature, caring model citizen like him) knocks on your door to take little Sally on a date, you can rest assured she is being escorted to her destination by a gentleman.

But seriously, who am I kidding? I can practically guarantee that there isn't going to be a model anything that comes reverently knocking at your door. Teenage boys like this are few and far between. The young man who'll show up to escort your daughter is likely going to be full of surging testosterone, and illegally acquired beer. He will also be blessed with the finger dexterity of a master magician, and the kind of night vision capabilities normally reserved for big cats.

His years thus far have likely been lacking a firm, caring role model, or even a half-decent father. In fact, where his dad is concerned, every fear you herald in regard to the worst personality type possible is well represented here! When this young hooligan's father *was* present, the examples set forth by this knuckle-dragging Neanderthal were a mixture of alcohol dependency and borderline personality disorder. It hasn't been a pretty example and now the youth is old enough to personally deliver his own brand of takeout right to your door.

Life is grand, isn't it?

But wait, before you despair and begin acquiring leg irons and a chain with which to secure your daughter in the far reaches of your basement, help is on the horizon.

I learned a few things during my four years with the British Royal Marine Commandos, and one of the most important lessons I garnered during that time is that if you plan for the worst and hope for the best, you'll rarely be caught unprepared. Thus I present to you this guide to interviewing and screening your daughter's boyfriends. I am going to teach you how to be a master interrogator of your daughter's dates, so you and she can work together to find her perfect match. Some of the things I'm going to share with you are:

- Why your ability to influence your daughter's dating choices begins long before she's old enough to date.

- Why building rapport with her boyfriend will aid the interview.
- How to accurately sum him up in ten minutes or less by scrutinizing the verbal and body language he uses.

Don't get me wrong, this book isn't the end-all answer to your dating concerns. If your daughter is inclined to reject your opinion or strike back at you, it won't matter how good your interrogation techniques are because she won't be listening to anything you have to say. That's the result of problems cultivated during her youth, when you were too busy to spend time with her and show her how a respectful, quality guy talks and acts.

If you and your daughter don't have good rapport, or if she doesn't take you and your guidance seriously, I would advise you to go ahead and surrender to the inevitable string of misfits she's going to bring home to meet you. Of course, moving your family to the outskirts of Nome, Alaska, might at least limit the number. Just a thought!

For now, let's presume that you have a stellar relationship with your daughter and only want her to be happy. If this is the case, then a blanket approach of "terrorize them all" will only result in scaring away the one she should be with. Good fathers want their daughters to be safe; great fathers want their daughters to be safe and happy.

To that end, I would like to form a partnership with you, at least for the duration of this book. Please raise your right hand and repeat after me, "I *(your name here)* do solemnly swear not to threaten, beat, intimidate, or hurt my daughter's dates until I have completed this book. I swear not to do this until I have all of the information I need to make an informed decision about who is deserving of an ass-beating and who is not." You should swear this oath in the name of your daughter's long-term happiness.

In the event that you discover a date is unsuitable for your daughter's fair hand, but you are unable to kick his ass alone, you will find the web address and phone number for the dads' club I have launched at the back of this book. If such a time comes, you will be able to procure substantial backup from our "group."

And speaking of not straying from the herd, so to speak, have you ever noticed how women never go anywhere alone, not even to the bathroom? This is why you won't see a girl leave the bathroom with toilet paper stuck to her shoe, or hanging unceremoniously from her nylons, something I myself have done—the shoe thing, not the nylons. Within the sisterhood, they would never allow such a travesty to happen. If all concerned fathers stick together like women do, then you, sir, will not be facing your daughter's coming of age alone, and more importantly, neither will I!

"Where did you go to receive your training on body language?"

This is one of the questions I often hear after my seminars and the answer comes in three parts. My childhood wasn't the worst in the world, but it was also a long way from being the best. My dad, God rest his soul, was prone to violent outbursts and exacted as much control over everyone and everything he could. Growing up with these sorts of antics was tough, but it granted me the sort of real-world human behavior education that cannot be replicated anywhere else. Any advance warning, and I could have helped lessen the emotional impact of an outburst, or attack, so I spent my entire childhood learning to pay attention to every facial and body language clue that I could. I might not have been able to do anything about the physical aspects of being hit, but at least seeing things coming was like having a small but powerful buffer from some of the emotional impact. It was these circumstances that delivered the first part of my body language training, and they lasted until I left home at seventeen.

During my time in the military I was fortunate enough to attend a variety of courses on human behavior and body language, and it was here that I realized I excelled at reading people. During one presentation the instructor began calling people up to the front of the room to answer questions. Once the unlucky bugger had finished answering the instructor's inquiries, the rest of the room discussed what they had seen or heard. I wasn't sure how to categorize the signals displayed, but according to the instructor I was extremely accurate at describing emotions and personality types. I was intrigued and couldn't get enough. After leaving the Commandos I enrolled in every course I could afford (and find time to attend) and soaked up the information like a sponge. Something unexpected occurred during this time, too.... I realized a sense of gratitude for my childhood experiences.

Over the years I have learned how difficult it is for people to observe and accurately interpret information in real time. Holding a conversation eats up the listener's ability to be attentive. Observing gestures, facial expressions, and listening wholeheartedly is a real challenge. Often, unless there is a personal or professional reason to pay special attention to the speaker, the focus tends to be watered down as we internalize what the speaker is saying and how we are going to respond.

One way to improve your body language reading (in addition to attending classes) is to watch TV interviews with the sound off. Watching without sound eliminates that pesky word thing that can distract us from discerning what interviewees are really thinking. Not that words aren't important. Mark McClish, a speaker, trainer, and author, is fond of repeating the mantra, "People say exactly what they mean," during his Law Enforcement Statement Analyses classes; and we shall delve into language and the manner in which words are said in Chapter Seven.

As you study body language, you may find that your circle of friends begins to shrink. I don't think you should worry about this. I know that's easy for me to say, as I don't know how few friends you have, but I've always believed in quality over quantity. This may happen because as you become more efficient at interpreting signals, you find some of your oldest friends are full of crap—or as I like to say, codswallop—are emotional basket cases, or enjoy oiling up and wearing diapers on a Friday night. On the positive side, if you discover they are full of codswallop, creating distance from them frees up backyard space during July Fourth celebrations and leaves more barbecue fare for everyone else.

In addition to thinning the friends herd, be warned, as your interpretation skills improve you may want to share what you learn with your kids. For the longest time I thought most of the information I was passing along to my kids in regard to body and verbal language assessments was falling on deaf ears; you may well understand what I mean when I say children's eyes sometimes glaze over when they suspect one of Dad's lectures is about to begin. Sometimes it's hard to tell whether anything I'm telling them is actually making it passed the vacant stare. So, you can imagine my surprise when a few weeks after one of my more interesting explanations about verbal pauses (latency response), when waiting for an answer, a question was thrown back at me. Cora (my eldest child, aged nine at the time) wanted to know when my wife and I started having "the sex." This was definitely a question that made me pause. My wife and I generally try to be as open and honest with our kids' questions (in an age-appropriate way, of course) as we can; but this was one of those rare times when it seemed the best course of action was to dance around the subject as quickly and smoothly as possible, and hopefully duck the guaranteed follow-up grilling. Yes, I was being a coward. I didn't want to tell an outright lie, so I stumbled through the following answer: "Mom and Dad have been married for a long time and love each other very much, and we waited until after we were married before we began to have sex." Here's how that answer played out:

Cora: "You paused a very long time before answering, Dad. And I didn't saying anything about marriage, I asked about the sex. You told me a lot. Are you telling the truth?"

Holy crap! I was busy doing ten other things and had my back to her during her response, and I'm glad I did, as I think my jaw bounced off my chest twice. I'd just been outdone by my nine-year-old! I was trapped somewhere between shock and awe and the deepest pride a father can feel. She had listened, and apparently very well. I was now jaw-flapping like a fish out of water and responded the only way I could think to: "Go ask your mother."

As soon as her back was turned I began feverishly texting her mother, hoping to provide some much-needed prep time before our precocious daughter ambushed her. I'm not clear how my wife heroically steered her way through the resulting interrogation; but suffice it to say, her mother and I vowed to get our stories straight on a variety of topics from that point forward. I also vowed to cease and desist sharing more decoding techniques. So be warned, most of what you teach your kids will bounce right off their armored noggins; but anything that can come back to bite you on the ass or cause you major panic will go right into the vault of eternal memory and be released when you least expect it.

"We are not human beings on a spiritual path, but spiritual beings on a human path."

—Jean Shinoda Bolen

I'd like to share with you where the idea for this book came from, and please don't let my confession affect your enthusiasm for reading on. It is, after all, the information the book contains, rather than where the idea came from, that is important.

Until the last few years I never would have said I was a big believer in fate, divine intervention, chance encounters, or any other mystical gobbledygook. I was a cynic—a pragmatist at best. But, oh boy, has that changed. Now I'm not about to try to convince you otherwise if you don't believe in any of that stuff. I was perfectly happy (at least I thought I was) not believing in much of anything and being highly suspicious of everyone outside a chosen few. I expect that if you don't believe in forces larger than yourself, it's easy to be happy behind whatever wall you surround yourself with. I was content behind my wall for many years. You may hide behind one for many more years, if not indefinitely, and if this is who you are, then no worries. But

I had a huge change in perspective. This change was due in part to my father's death, by suicide, in 2008.

My father was an angry, dark person who was rarely able to enjoy the lighter side of life. Following his passing, I felt myself slipping into the same sort of mind-set he had. Few things made me happy. My wife strived to keep everything together, while I did less and less. Then, when I think I had exhausted her last reserve, she took a chance and paid for me to consult a psychic medium. I'm not sure why a medium (as opposed to a therapist), but I think my wife wanted me to connect with my dad and get more answers than I could garner from the books I was reading. The medium, whom I had never met before and had been given only my first name, relayed information to me that no one else knew. She described events from my childhood, listing specific things that I hadn't told anyone. She gave me a huge psychic kick to the tenders and woke me up. Talk about a shock—I was majorly unsettled!

Then the psychic explained that I needed to write a book. I countered that a few years prior I had been writing a book on self-leadership. I further explained that I had written more than 120 pages when my computer contracted a virus and ate the damn thing. Even the external hard drive backup had gone. There wasn't a way in hell I was starting that over again. And yes, the irony about my having almost written a book about self-motivation, never giving up, and then walking away from my project when all of it vanished, isn't lost on me either. It didn't help my nerves when I told the medium this and she calmly replied that the universe knows when the time is right or wrong, and that that book wasn't the one I was supposed to be writing—at least not at the time. I was, as you can imagine, about to explode with frustration. She had touched on one too many soft spots. I angrily asked her what the hell I was supposed to be writing about, even listing body language for cops as a possible topic, and she said she didn't think that should be the subject either, or at least not exactly. She then chuckled and said I will know it when I know it, as the "universe" was already aligning to provide me with the answer.

What the hell does "the universe is aligning" mean? I felt like the "universe" and I were about to come to blows! Even though the reading shocked me, referencing truths I had turned my back on long ago, I wasn't fully ready to jump on board with this mystic mumbo jumbo. All I could think was, WTF! But she was right, it was aligning. I was already teaching how to read body language at locations around the country, but these sessions were aimed toward improving communication for corporate personnel, improving interview techniques, and recognizing dangerous nonverbal signals for law enforcement. A book specifically written to help dads navigate meeting and screening their daughter's dates hadn't occurred to me. That was going to change.

Over the course of half a dozen presentations, I was approached by various attendees and received similar messages: "I wish you could be with me when I meet my daughter's boyfriends" and "You should write a book about screening boyfriends." The last straw occurred a few days after my family and I relocated to Jackson Hole, Wyoming, when the first person I was introduced to, another dad, made a similar remark when he learned what I did for a living. He said, "I wish I could have you and your people-reading skills next to me when my daughter starts dating. It would be crazy good to have you help me weed out the losers. Hey, maybe you could write a book." Is this seriously happening again? I wondered. Then, okay, universe, I'm listening.

I can be a quick learner in some matters and dense as a fencepost in others. But even I realized that after a year of this happening over and over again, someone, somewhere, was trying to tell me something. Much to my surprise, the psychic was right.

Ultimately the universe aligned and the message got through. I was inspired by all of the dads making similar comments. I want to be with them, with you, when your daughter brings home her latest flame—and not just so we can comfort one another once he walks out the door with her. I'd like to begin a revolution wherein dads get to play an active role in helping select Mr. Right; because for far too long we've had to sit on the sidelines because our behavior has been less than helpful. Too often we approach interactions with new boyfriends like a proverbial bull in a china shop, glaring and intimidating our way through our time with them, but accomplishing very little that is constructive. Not surprisingly, your daughter may have come to expect you to act this way, and so plans accordingly, ensuring your time with the new boyfriend is kept as brief as possible.

Once you finish this book, you will know why your role in helping your daughter find true happiness begins long before she starts dating. Why even if you have only a few minutes with him, you'll be able to recognize future asshole conduct, or worse, dangerous impulses, and do something about them. You'll be able to articulate what you've seen and move yourself from a sideline observer to the centerfield star. And maybe, just maybe, you won't have to suffer through holiday weekend family reunions with a son-in-law whom you'd like to strangle every time you cross paths. Consider a world where Mom's happy because she isn't having to stress you'll do or say something bad during your short time with him. Your daughter can trust you're on her side when it comes to her finding her soul mate. And even you will enjoy being around him. That's a multiple-win situation and no one has to die to get there. So let's get cracking, as none of us are getting any younger and your daughter's love selection hangs precariously in the balance.

CHAPTER TWO

Circle of Trust

> "I have found that the best way to give advice to your children is to find out what they want and then advise them to do it."
>
> —Harry S. Truman

- Rubber gloves
- Electronic cattle prod
- Good pair of pliers
- Eighteen-volt cordless drill
- Unpadded metal chair in a soundproof room in the basement

"Yes, dear, Daddy is now ready to meet your new boyfriend." Yeah, right! If only it was this easy! The amount of post-incident paperwork that would accompany this type of interrogation is nearly enough to make you not want to do it.... Nearly. But it will make things very challenging when discussing where the date went after he flees. So there has to be another way, and there is; it's called waterboarding and involves a bathtub half filled with ice-cold water, a cotton T-shirt, and a dressing gown cord to secure his wrists without leaving marks.

I'm just beginning to realize I might have given this scenario too much consideration. Waterboarding isn't "legal" for enemy combatants, so I'm pretty sure I won't be allowed to subject my daughters' dates to such measures.

My daughter Cora was born at thirty-three weeks and spent her first two weeks in the NICU for observation. She was subjected to regular blood tests in order to monitor her iron levels, among other things. She never cried when they jabbed her heel to take the sample, and even the nurses who administered the test were impressed by this. They'd comment to my wife and me, "She's doing great. She's tough as nails and hasn't cried once."

All I could think while the tests were being run was that no one would ever hurt my little girl again. If it's possible to feel more than the normal amount of parental protectiveness over a newborn, her time in the NICU achieved it. The only way I was able to control the urge to strangle the perpetrators of those tests was by consoling myself with the fact that they were doing this for her benefit. They were providing the twenty-four-hour care needed for a preemie, and without them, she might not have made it. I remember watching her sleep inside the incubator. She was so tiny she could fit in the palm of my hand. I couldn't believe someone so small could be so resilient.

Thankfully, Cora suffered no complications as a result of being premature and has grown into a feisty, sporty, and beautiful young lady with a slight tomboy edge and mild dislike for anything too girly, at least for now. Looking back, though, I realize that during her time in the hospital, I never considered the time might arrive when she would be old enough to begin dating. The same is true for both my girls. I thought they'd always be kids and forever need my protection.

It's common knowledge that daughters expect their dads to be picky when it comes to their dating choices. What's needed is a complete shift in the way dads deliberate over potential suitors for their girls. You have to know that there is someone out there good enough for her, and more importantly, so must your little girl. If your daughter knows that you are helping her find the right guy, then she knows the two of you are working toward the same end, her happiness. If this happens, she is more likely to work with you than against you. But if you have already made it clear that no one will ever measure up to your expectations, she already knows that her boyfriends, both good and bad, will all receive the same treatment. So why should she take your opinion into consideration?

This could present a problem for you, Dad, as it means she might be inclined to bring home one of two types of boys: a work-in-progress boyfriend, or a disaster/revenge boyfriend. The first choice might not be too bad. According to 99 percent of women around the free world (I took a survey) all men are works in progress, the only thing up in the air is the degree of improvement they need to make. As long as she has set high standards for herself, your daughter's choice may require minimal work. But, she could just as easily choose guys who require massive amounts of improvement because she likes the challenge. The added bonus is the passive aggressive way she can strike back at you by bringing home such a guy. Looking on the bright side, if she knows that there is room for improvement, large or small, she will probably discuss this with one of the following:

A. Her friends
B. Her mother
C. The family dog, her friends, and her mother

Please note that you are not among those listed as trusted confidants. Your general ill will toward all her boyfriends has evicted you from the circle of trust. If you want input in the selection of your daughter's dates, boyfriends, or, dare I say, husband, you have got to remain inside the circle of trust! Your skills in reading and interpreting her boyfriend's behavior will be for naught if no one listens to what you are saying. You must make yourself part of the team and the cost of admission will be your acceptance of her goal: the procurement of a weak, mindless fool who will follow her every command to the letter. No, no… I'm joking, of course. She likely doesn't really want that kind of mate, and neither will you want that for her. Who the hell wants a husband or son-in-law with no balls? But if you want to make sure he has the right kind of balls, you've got to be in the loop from the beginning. You can't jump in late in the game as a substitute referee and think the players will start listening. If you do this, you'll be received as a lunatic outsider with no idea what's been transpiring thus far in the competition. There is no room for a Monday morning quarterback in this championship match. If you're in, then you're in, and she will need to know that so you never end up outside the circle.

I'm sure I don't have to explain the meaning of a disaster/revenge boyfriend. But just in case, I'll cover it in broad terms. This guy's an asshole plain and simple. I'm not talking about a pretend, wannabe asshole either. I mean the real deal. You should resign yourself to the fact that your daughter is going to date at least one bad boy, even if just for comparison's sake. She has to kiss a lot of frogs to find a prince—at least that's what my wife keeps telling me. But I'm not sure it's making me feel better….

Well, this guy isn't a frog, he's a wolf. He is your worst-case scenario. He will be nearly impossible to intimidate because his life thus far has been one ass-kicking after another. Dad handed him enough beatings during the early years of his life that now nothing short of pulling his fingernails out is going to slow this low-life down. Even your daughter doesn't really like him. So why is she with him? Because of you!

With a revenge boyfriend, your daughter thinks she is sticking it to you. And in a way, she is—but only partly. You and I both know that ultimately she is the one who will pay the price. But we dads will still have to be there to help pick up the pieces when it all goes wrong, if she'll let us. This type of boyfriend and resulting scenario is the one we are trying to avoid at all costs. We do not want her so mad at us for our shortfalls that this fool becomes an attractive proposition. He is the reason we must never relegate ourselves to the outside of the trusted circle of confidants. The price to stay inside isn't steep. All it entails are:

1. Being willing to talk to her about everything (including sex).
2. Taking time to bond with her on a regular basis (her sense of self-worth is on the line if you don't).
3. Letting her know that you are just as interested in her finding Mr. Right as she is.

That isn't too bad a price to pay, is it? You've probably heard the expression, "If you think paying for an education is expensive, try not getting one." If you think the above fees are a tad high or too difficult to achieve with your work and golf schedule, try skipping this tariff and see how sky-high the costs go. You will be devastated.

This brings us to one of the most difficult challenges a dad faces when it comes to his daughter's boyfriends: bonding with them. Bonding with your daughter's boyfriends will afford you more intelligence-gathering opportunities than playing badass will, even if the latter course of action is infinitely more appealing.

First form a plan of attack, or more accurately, a plan of counterattack mixed with a little guerrilla warfare. A full frontal assault will only alienate your daughter.

I'm fortunate in that I have a slight advantage over most fathers. All my kids have grown up thinking I can practically read their minds, and that information is worth its weight in gold, especially when my girls start dating. Among their friends this skill is both a curiosity and a threat. I've heard my daughters tell their friends, "Don't lie to my dad, he'll know!"

All my kids learned early on that if I call them into a room to ask questions about something they might have done, I'm going to know within seconds whether or not they're answering honestly. Now a part of this skill is based on the formal training I received in this arena, but some of this ability is derived from the time I've spent bonding with them and learning their mannerisms. Every minute I have spent hanging with my kids—hiking, building forts, wrestling, helping with homework, listening to the recaps of their days at school, tickle fights, playing catch, teaching them to ride bikes—all of it was bonding, and, of course, research. There is no substitute for time spent together. And if you are going to commit to that time, then you might as well dedicate some of your efforts to learning their gestures, facial nuances, and idiosyncratic quirks—and the insight these can provide into what your kid is really thinking.

One difference between kids and adults is that kids have yet to develop the sort of emotional baggage that grown-ups are saddled with. Where kids' body language is concerned, it is usually much more innocent and uncomplicated. Adults are much more complicated. If there is a gap between an adult's public and private facade there can be disparity in how they present themselves to the world around them. If someone has deep, dark secrets they will be echoed in strange, idiosyncratic behavior. In other words, the more problems a person has, the weirder they become to folks around them.

Now don't go rolling your eyes, fearing I'm about to go off on some tirade about how everyone is psychologically scarred and suffering from major Daddy issues. In that regard, it's safer to assume everyone has them, and then those who don't will pleasantly surprise you. You need to know this because this will provide insight into how we interrogate—I mean interview—our daughters' dates. Remember, this isn't about your issues—God knows we don't have time for that discussion—this is about the boyfriend's problems and the ways that we must interact with him in order to uncover how deep the rabbit warren runs.

Typically, the greater the amount of emotional baggage, the greater the chance that there will be incongruences between what is said and what is shown nonverbally. You might not always consciously recognize the odd behavior that sets your alarm bells ringing, but something about the person in question unsettles you. My goal is for you to be able to identify the signals of a boyfriend who has issues, classify them, and then coherently and sympathetically report your reading to those who matter, i.e., your daughter and wife. I say sympathetically because if your end-goal is to warn your daughter to stay away from certain boyfriend personality traits, you don't want her feeling sorry for him when you refer to him as a basket case. You also don't want to blurt out halfway through your meet-and-greet that he should be shot and buried during the next full moon. You must present your observations as a caring human being, only reporting information for the benefit of those around you. Never share your findings from a position of judgment or ill will, regardless of how ill your will really is. You have to keep that to yourself. If your assessment is to carry weight with your daughter, she must trust that what you are telling her comes from the purest of places, void of bias or the threat of large pointy sticks.

The level of trust depends largely on the open, honest conversations you and your daughter have had up until that point. It's never easy to find time for one-on-one conversations, or time to bond. Between work and regular family obligations, most of us don't have time to spit. But making time, even the smallest amount, can have a huge impact on your relationship with your daughter, and more specifically on the degree of trust you share. If finding time up until this moment has been tough and still seems overwhelming, don't sweat it. It doesn't have to be a huge song and dance. Ten minutes here and there will be worth its weight in gold. I suggest you begin with things you know she likes to do or talk about. For example, all of my kids enjoy outdoor activities, but my girls especially like a trip to the local coffee shop to play chess and hang out. Aidan can't sit still, so for him it's anything that involves serious activity, and if things blow up or go *bang,* all the better! On the occasions when I've taken either of my girls for a walk or to the coffee shop, they are completely content after thirty to sixty minutes. At that point, they've said everything they want to say and are beaming from ear to ear. No matter which girl I am hanging out with, I take every opportunity during these excursions to hold the door for her, tell her how smart and pretty she is (in that order), and generally treat her like a lady at every opportunity.

On hikes with my girls, I take the time to teach them how to build a shelter, navigate with a compass, know what's safe to eat, and even use a knife. Whether hacking at dead tree branches to get wood for a fire or practicing defensive and offensive implementation of the blade to disarm an attacker (my favorite), there is always something that can be shared and discussed. It was during one of my knife lessons that I found out Cora isn't a fan of blood, or in this case even the discussion of it. I went easy on the gory details of using a knife for defense and instead focused on the point of the knife lesson, having fun and bonding.

My younger daughter, Sophie, also likes to hike, and often outlasts her siblings. She is soft-spoken and I have had to work at being patient when she talks so quietly that I can barely hear her. She is also the biggest carnivore in the family, and the sight of blood doesn't bother her in the least. After asking me to kill a squirrel for her to eat (yep, she asked for it), she took the most time investigating the insides of the furry critter before chowing down on its grilled carcass. Along with her sister and brother, she is a crack shot. If she could hunt every day of her life and live on steak, she'd be in petite princess heaven.

One other thing I'd like you to consider incorporating as part of the open communication component of your relationship with your daughter is the sex talk. This is never easy, I don't care how prepared you are. When Cora asked me the sex question I mentioned to you earlier, I instinctively tried dodging the question rather than answering it, and her mother and I had already covered the basics with her. I think because her question was personal I was caught off guard. Nor did I have the luxury of spending two hours psyching up before answering her question, in the same way as I had done when my wife and I had first talked about things with her. There is no subject more unsettling for a father to broach with his daughter, but this book isn't about your feelings. Well, not exactly. It's about cultivating an intelligent young lady who has a male role model she can trust at every twist and turn of her life, and sex can be a very treacherous path without the proper guidance.

Now, there are books galore out there with a variety of opinions on when is the right time to talk with your kids about sex. This is something you and your wife should decide together. Mom should also be with you when this discussion happens, especially for the first time, and the two of you should present a united front in terms of how sex is discussed and referenced. The two of you need to be clear on how the topic is delivered and how you both intend to answer the questions that will follow. If you fight during the discussion, you may cause your daughter to be more confused than when it began. If she starts forming opinions about what "sex" means because of how you two carry on in front of her, then you two might sully her view of it for the rest of her life. If this happens, you may inadvertently push her one step closer to a life of using a pseudonym at the local gentlemen's club.

As for the timing of the much-dreaded talk, I advocate using common sense, but suggest sooner rather than later—especially given the amount of information passed to her by her friends, or readily available online. I think it's best to have the discussion, utilizing age-appropriate language and terminology, when she mentions something that requires addressing and not ignoring. A factor in my wife and I deciding to have our first sex talk with our then eight-year-old was the odd things she began to say at home. Nearly all the eyebrow-raising comments were completely out of character for her, and they worried us tremendously. We had been careful to monitor computer time, TV time, and the books she read. The things we couldn't control were her time on the school bus or at school with older kids who presumably weren't being as well shielded as our kids were.

There's not much you can do about schoolyard comments, except be prepared to explain what "blow me" really means (or your version). Our explanation revolved around a theme of dynamite and bodily harm—something I wanted to brandish on the reprobate who used this sort of language around younger kids. I'll tell you from experience, it's a lot easier to answer many of their questions if you've already opened up the floor to calm, sensible straight talk about sex. Unless they ambush you with questions about your own history, then by all means, bob and weave like a champ.

If you aren't prepared or haven't launched a discussion, there's a good chance you'll fumble your way through your answers, probably making a dog's dinner of it. You'll ultimately make your child so uncomfortable with your stammering that she'll regret asking you. At which time, she'll begin getting her information from people a lot less self-conscious, and certainly less scrupulous—her friends.

If you haven't already, you should resign yourself to the fact that your daughter will be exposed to a form of "sex education" from her peers at some horrendously early time in her life, whether you like it or not; so choose to be the source of clarity. My advice is for you to put your big-boy panties on and suck it up. You're her dad and you've already admitted you'd commit a felony for her (I'm pretty sure that's how the Feds would view your kidnapping and torturing that punk down the road), so why not go the extra mile and do something really useful: provide her with as much unbiased straight talk about life as you are capable of providing.

During your sex talk, you should be studying her behavior. Every nuance and slip of nonverbal information is a golden nugget for the vault. Reading her will become harder and harder as she ages, if for no other reason than because life will teach her how to mask emotions to protect herself. You need to master interpreting her signals if you want to be able to decode what she might not be keen to tell you sometime down the road.

If I've taught you anything so far, it should be that bonding comes in all forms and with a little advance planning doesn't have to be a painful experience for either of you. It is of paramount importance that she recognizes that your interest in her boyfriends is not some power play to meddle in her life or stifle her maturity and strive for independence. She has to know that you are interested in all aspects of her life and that you are most definitely on her side when it comes to her finding Mr. Right. Even if, like me, just saying those words are enough to make you choke with disdain, resign yourself to the fact that it's her feelings that count and our own issues need to get the hell out of the way.

Personally, I have had to work hard to not minimize my kids' concerns and feelings. Let's face it, as men we aren't naturally inclined to think of our children's problems as being very serious. After all, we have shielded them and will continue to shield them from real-world issues like paying bills, being attacked, or starving to death. But we do need to understand that our sons' and daughters' issues are important *to them*. Our issues may seem more serious than theirs, but for them they matter—and we always need to keep that in mind.

So what type of personality does your daughter have? Do you have any idea what sorts of boyfriends she's most likely to want to date? Does she already have a type? I know that at twelve, Cora does. Ten-year-old Sophie is beginning to form opinions, too. Cora's type falls somewhere between sporty and nerdy—in equal measure. And Sophie likes "ab muscles" and motorcycles, so with her I'm bracing for the worst.

Having at least some idea of what kind of young man will be gracing your doorstep will be a huge help in predicting how much of a problem he is likely to be. There is a reason for stereotypes, so be aware that if a bad-boy rocker type appeals to your daughter, he may have various shortcomings, and your approach to interviewing him should take this into account.

If your daughter does share what type of boy she likes, it might be a good idea to not mention what you plan to do with that information. If she thinks you might be capitalizing on personal information in order to read him more efficiently, she might start keeping it to herself. One more reason to spend quality time with her asking questions about everything that goes on in her life is to help smooth the way for you to inquire about her boyfriend. After all, you ask questions about a multitude of different subjects, so she knows this isn't anything Machiavellian—it's just you being you! Good old curious Dad. He wants to know his daughter as well as he can. So this is just one more topic in a broad array of things that you ask questions about. It's all perfectly normal.

M. E. Thomas wrote in her book *Confessions of a Sociopath*, "People are so hungry for love; they die a little every day for want of it—for want of touch and acceptance." But if as a child, your daughter is getting these things, it decreases the likelihood of her having a desperate need for them in her adult years. If she knows unconditional parental love, then she is less likely to fall for the manipulations of someone trying to con her into a harmful relationship. And validation and teachings from her dad can carry twice the weight they would than if they came from someone else in her life, especially when it comes to shaping how she views the world and her role in it.

Of course, no matter what you intend to teach her, if she observes that you and your wife don't value one another, then everything you are trying to do for her might be for naught. You might think that how you treat your wife, her mother, and how your daughter views herself are completely separate relationships, but they aren't. You may want your daughter to soak up everything you share with her about self-assurance, independence, happiness, love, respect, etc., but if she's seeing you belittle, marginalize, or generally disregard her mother, or another female role model, then she may project that negativity onto herself. What you say to her will have little impact on her development if what she observes undermines those lessons. You can't ask her to heed your words when your actions have guided her emotions to opposite conclusions about how a woman should be treated.

If, on the other hand, you treat Mom like a queen—respecting and valuing her opinions, hugging and displaying affection toward her, laughing and hanging out with her, bringing her flowers for no apparent reason—this will all support the lessons you've been giving her. If your actions are harmonious with what she is hearing, then, holy crap, mate, you will have done more to ensure your daughter makes smart dating choices than with anything else—and your job screening boyfriends will be considerably easier.

In the next chapter, we are going to figure out who you are and what makes you tick, and gently steer you toward the proper way to interview Junior when you meet him. We'll cover ways you can build rapport with him quickly—so that as his anxiety decreases, your ability to accurately assess him increases. Once he is relaxed, you'll be in a position to ask tough questions and get a pretty decent measure of the lad.

CHAPTER THREE

Rapport

> "He will win who knows when to fight and when not to fight."
>
> —Sun Tzu

All right, let's talk about you. Yes, I know this doesn't happen very often, if ever these days, but close your mouth and stop looking so surprised. You knew that eventually we'd have to consider who you really are, and although this doesn't mean we are going to start taking long showers together in the wee hours, I do need to understand what makes you tick. More importantly, so do you. Now, traditionally, we men aren't too good when it comes to self-analyses, or even moderate self-criticism. And why would we be? We are perfect just the way we are… right? Err, *no*. I hate to be the conveyer of bad news, but you come with a shitload of baggage. Everything you've probably heard from your wife over the last six thousand years is dead-on. And no, you don't have to tell her that. It'll be our little secret.

Now that we've established this new bond, I'd like you to ask yourself, what kind of a man is your daughter's father? What makes him mad or happy? How does he carry himself? What kinds of people does he get along with best, or worst? What clothes does he wear? Is he active? Does he have hobbies? Is he sarcastic and jovial, or mean and grumpy, or does he not have any of these attributes? Is he emotional or reserved? Controlling or laid-back? Is he an observer, studious and careful in his observations, or brazen and take-charge with little time for subtleties or patience? Or is he a combination of all of these things, depending on the circumstances and people around him?

Take a few minutes to think about yourself. Don't think about yourself as you would like to be thought of, think about yourself as you really are. Who are you? Consider which life events and experiences most shaped who you are. Do they involve things done to you, or by you? If I've managed to get you to commit to a few moments of introspection, I'll count my lucky stars. And now, I'll begin by explaining why those moments in your life are so important.

Everything that has happened in your life has affected what kind of person you are. How you walk, talk, stand, dress, and even laugh have been molded by events and experiences. When you meet your daughter's boyfriend, all of these events and experiences will be meeting him, too.

So ask yourself, how much does he have to fear?

You must know yourself well because I just heard you proudly declare, "He should be extremely afraid!" But he shouldn't be overly afraid; it will make him too anxious (granted when meeting the father for the first time there *should* always be a little trepidation, that's completely normal). But you shouldn't want him stressed so badly that the signals he shows during the meeting make it hard to get an accurate reading of who he truly is.

Let's take a moment to revisit those boyhood fantasies of yours (no, not *those* fantasies). Pretend you are a seasoned detective in a real-life game of cops and robbers. Now I'm not referring to the "old-school sweats," often portrayed on television shows. We aren't interested, or shouldn't be interested, in impersonating the sort of cop who beats admissions out of suspects, regardless of how much more interesting that makes the character. I'd like you to be the veteran cop, whose attention to detail, amazing tenacity, and unnerving ability to place himself inside the mind of a criminal are what result in his cases being solved. In this activity, you need to forget CSI. Think of yourself as solving cases by being a human interacting with another human, and reading and relating to that individual at his or her level. That requires mad skills, patience, and the ability to observe and listen in a relaxed manner, to avoid unnerving the suspect.

Unlike the American legal system, which embraces a presumption of innocence until proven guilty, we, as fathers, must operate on the expectation that our daughters' dates are guilty until proven innocent. I guarantee they've done something bad in the past, so the only thing up in the air is their level of guilt! We must figure out how bad and whether it's bad enough to be an indicator of possible future infractions that might affect your daughter. We must also be savvy enough to interrogate them in a manner that doesn't raise red flags (for them), while at the same time allowing our powers of observation and deduction to uncover shortfalls or areas of sensitivity. In poker we might refer to such emotional leaks as "tells," but I prefer to think of them in broader terms, as we are looking for ANY emotion outside of his normally displayed ones. For this reason, I prefer the phrase "hotspot" to describe emotional reactivity to your questions, regardless of whether his leak is happy, sad, mad, surprised, contemptuous, or a combination of them all. We are interested in any sentiment he might suddenly experience, and will categorize it as an emotional leak, or "hotspot" for short.

I know that all of this might not seem fair or just. In fact, when you say it aloud, all of the conspiring and scheming sounds dirty. Are we really going to try to manipulate the poor kid into saying or doing something that might reveal his shortcomings, past bad deeds, or insecurities? DAMN RIGHT! Now quit feeling guilty, you're making me misty.

Before you begin grilling the poor S.O.B., you need him to relax. Don't let him catch on that you know he's guilty of something. I don't want him more guarded than he'll already be because he's meeting his girlfriend's dad. I certainly don't want him to clam up and bring his A-game poker face because this will only make our lives harder!

I want the young man relaxed, and, dare I say, confident. Just like the wily detective, I know that if he's in a laid-back state of mind, there's a better chance he'll give straight answers (and nonverbal signals) that you can use to build a portfolio of information.

But before you begin scrutinizing his nonverbal signals and body language, you need to spend a little time analyzing your own. If you think this is going to be difficult, ask your wife for help. I'm sure she'll tell you in no uncertain terms about every minute detail of the things you do that are antisocial, annoying, or intimidating. If she says you come across as an asshole (in the nicest possible way), believe her. If she hints you couldn't intimidate a preschooler, also believe her. Cut back on the origami (unless you can fashion a throwing star out of heavyweight cardboard) and start lifting weights, or wrestling crocs, because at some point you might have to man up and defend your daughter, especially if he comes calling after she's decided to end things. Note, though, that if you aren't naturally scary, this could in some ways work to your advantage, at least at first. Nothing helps relax a future boyfriend quicker than a dad who looks like he squeals at the sight of blood. But eventually you'll need to work on an image overhaul in order to present a more masculine facade. As a sidenote, what you wear can help cultivate the right impression, without excessively putting the young lad on edge. For instance, if you love golf shirts, and I'm sure a lot of you do, save them for impressing your golf buddies at the club. Golf shirts, along with "slacks" and Hugh Hefner slippers, tasseled shoes, or Birkenstocks, couldn't imply less danger than if you wore a dress to your first meeting. And unless you look like, or better yet, actually *are* Daniel Craig in a *James Bond* movie, you should also skip the dress shirt and sports coat.

I've now got half of you reconsidering two-thirds of your wardrobe, so what should you wear? It will be best to don a pair of well-fitting jeans, your old AC/DC T-shirt (as long as it still fits; once again ask your wife because if she can't suppress a titter at your expense, you better buy one that isn't stretched around your middle), and a good old-fashioned pair of outdoor boots or tennis shoes. And for the love of all things holy, don't pick up a pair of those white walking shoes that have a rounded sole to increase comfort. Nothing screams you are decrepit faster than geriatric shoes. Think work boots, hunting boots, or even cross-training ones for that "I just finished my third run up a mountainside" look.

For those of you who normally dress like a badass, be aware that less is more. If you hit the weights ten times a week and think spray-on Under Armour garments best display your girth, try to find a shirt large enough that it doesn't look like it belongs to your wife. Nothing echoes your insecurities and need to intimidate more effectively than skin-tight clothing wrapped around a body chock-full of steroids. How you communicate, both verbally and nonverbally, from the clothes you wear to the hobbies you enjoy and talk about, will impact how quickly you put him at ease—or scare the crap out of him. If you can modify or fine-tune your current image, so you don't scare him right away, but still resemble a guy's guy, you'll procure a more accurate understanding of his usual behavior.

Beyond clothing, one of the immediate things that will set a basis for his level of comfort is your handshake. Most of us consider the handshake used during an introduction to be of paramount importance, and to a degree it is. As an initial point of physical contact, this action is the most widely accepted Western greeting. All of us have experienced handshakes that put us at ease, or on edge. I've also had handshakes that were akin to grabbing hold of a wet kipper. Their touch was so flaccid and disturbing that I felt the need to decontaminate from the waist up. If the goal of their first impression was to make me feel as if I should be kissing their hand, rather than shaking it, they succeeded!

On the other end of the spectrum, there's the guy so desperate to prove his self-worth that he is in danger of herniating a disc by squeezing the offered hand as hard as humanly possible. This person's eyeballs bulge, and occasionally one can observe his tongue protruding from between his teeth in concentration. For those of you who use and think you are making a point with the "herniator handshake," you are correct. But it's probably not the one you want to make. It screams of insecurity and a desire to be feared.

The only type of handshake worse than the herniator is the "grappler." The guy who uses this isn't satisfied with merely trying to crush the bones in your hand. He wants to pull you off your feet and prove you are no match for his hand-and-arm strength. When I experience this, I have an overwhelming urge to dig my heels in and give him a run for his money. In greetings, a firm, but not excessively firm, handshake with a vertical thumb position and eye contact will suffice—unless you want to mess with him, in which case grapple away.

Things we sometimes overlook during an initial meeting and thereby cause the lad to be a wee bit overwhelmed are:

1. Things that might have been said in his pre-meeting talk with your daughter
2. The environment you meet him in
3. Your physical actions

In regard to his pre-meeting talk with your daughter, try to find out what your daughter told him about you. We all know this conversation happened and it is important to consider what might have been shared, as this will impact his state of mind.

What if you were meeting the father? What kind of information would you like to know, or not know, beforehand? What you discover could be unnerving or empowering. For instance, he might dread finding out that you collect poison blow-darts from all over the world, which, by the way, is one of my favorite hobbies. If you have acquired a similar interest, I recommend toxins from the Golden Poison Dart Frog *(Phyllobates terribilis)* or ones favored by the Choco Indians of Colombia. Be sure to alert your daughter well before she starts dating if you, too, have this kind of hobby. This will help keep

Junior in line and save you the inconvenience of having to bury him in the back garden.

On the other hand, he would probably love to know that you are an avid collector of coins. Why? Because hearing that you collect century-old metal relics as a pastime makes you sound as dangerous as a geriatric with a walker. Have you ever met a dangerous coin collector? I haven't. If coin collecting is your only hobby, I recommend cashing one of your more valuable sets in for a bodyguard service to chaperone your daughter. It might be the only way to keep her safe.

Consider what my daughters could tell their boyfriends:

"My dad is a former Royal Marine Commando (British Green Beret) who spent fifteen years post-military service teaching self-defense, kickboxing, knife fighting, and tactical gun utilization. He is now an instructor for law enforcement officers, among others professionals, improving how they read body language, interview suspects, and predict danger. He also competed on *Top Shot*, a show on the History Channel featuring the best marksmen in the country. Oh, and he wrote a book about how to interview, assess, and occasionally terrorize boyfriends."*

If I'd heard this résumé as a young man about to meet the "old man" for the first time, I'd have been nervous. Hell, unless I'd intended to marry the girl, I might not have gone near him. In considering your own résumé, compile a list of all the manly or dangerous things you do, or have done, and then sit and have a conversation with your daughter to be sure she is aware of them. Some things to consider:

---

* *Disclaimer: In regular conversation, I would never be so gratuitous with my history. But one day my future son-in-law might read this book, and I want him to know who he's dealing with if he ever hurts one of my girls.*

1. Do you work with your hands (preferably building skyscrapers without a safety harness)?
2. Do you hunt (something other than squirrels or your neighbor's obnoxious cat), and go "all the time"?
3. Do you fix your own truck or car? (It's better if it's a truck, for obvious reasons.)
4. Do you teach ninjas how to be better ninjas? (I'm trying to help you here.)

Share whatever is on your list. If necessary, embellish it with a daring story that your daughter will find amusing and exciting. This way, she is more likely to want to share your audacious exploits with you-know-who. Of course, if you have no daring exploits to tell of, or worse yet, are still warmly retelling your fraternity hazing experiences, then you are shit out of luck. Do not, I repeat, do not tell her that your claim to danger is that one time you attended a Tae Bo class and had to leave because you pulled a muscle. If you're realizing now that you need to launch a brand-new repertoire of hobbies, do it quickly.

It is preferable for the boyfriend to learn of your daring adventures through a third party, like your daughter, as very little you could say to him face-to-face is going to impact his psyche. If you start tooting your own horn, it'll come across as BS machismo and he'll let the information roll off his back like water off a duck's you-know-what. So let someone else share your exploits.

It's important that the shared information has at least a grain of truth to it, so you aren't left with your jaw flapping like a land-locked fish when he asks about "your" adventures. If the stories of your exploits are 100 percent true, then just ensure your daughter doesn't miss any pertinent facts. Retelling the important parts of the stories is crucial—otherwise why tell the stories at all?

The last thing you want is for the boyfriend to feel he's having his chain pulled. If this happens, you'll be the one looking like a goober, and you'll never establish the sort of bond where he'll be straight up with you about anything.

Environmental Considerations and *Your* Body Language

Environmental considerations are important because people tend to behave differently on their home turf, sometimes significantly so, than they do in unfamiliar settings. Typically, the farther we get from a familiar environment, the more unsettled we become. This is quadrupled when we meet a girlfriend's parents in their home. If the boyfriend is smart, he'd ask to meet the parents for the first time in a public location, cutting their home-court advantage.

If despite the home-court advantage, you are miffed that you're going to have to meet the boyfriend and make nice, then chances are your body language is going to be horrible. It could range from grotesquely superior to downright withdrawn, or plain pissed off. More than likely, it will be a combination of these. This is why it is important to acknowledge the potential of this before the introduction, and make a special effort to avoid it.

The main problem in overly stressing him out is that many of the nonverbal signs of distress are the same as the ones that might indicate deception. I wish I could tell you that there's only one signal that you need to know if he's lying, but then *I'd* be lying. In most cases, it will be a cluster of things that let you know something's amiss—and even then, you won't know if he is lying per se, you'll only know his anxiety level (an emotional hotspot) has increased and further questioning is required.

In order to aid yourself in distinguishing a fear of meeting you from the physiological responses to answering your questions with lies, you're going to need to eliminate as many unnecessary variables as possible. Intimidation, even good old-fashioned misguided "accidental" fear-mongering, must be avoided if you don't want to cloud the goal of reading him. Ultimately, we want him to pass your tests with flying colors. We don't want him to fail because if your daughter brings home one misfit after another, something has gone horribly wrong. It will signify that you haven't raised her with the ability to pursue respectable romantic partners.

There's one more catch: if he is a natural bullshitter and completely comfortable talking out of his ass, then many physiological signs of his doing it will be missing. If this becomes apparent, you'll need to use clever questioning and amazing listening skills to help illuminate his character flaws. More on this in Chapter Nine.

At the end of the day, we all process a lot of nonverbal information—sometimes consciously, but mostly subconsciously—seeking to discover whether the person we are interacting with poses a threat. Dads are at the top of the food chain as far as boyfriends are concerned. The boyfriend might already fear that his life could be over or that he could at least suffer moderate physical harm if the meeting doesn't go well. That fear, however, won't stop him from what he might try to do later with your young lass. That fear never stopped us, did it? But for now, he's interested in getting in and out of your house without ending up as a side dish to some fava beans and a nice bottle of Chianti.

It is your skills and cunning ways that will delay his escape and afford you the time needed to gather the requisite intelligence. Then, armed with the conclusions of your observations, you may either rest easy during her date or begin prepping the night-vision scope and that long-distance rifle you own. Of course, I'm kidding.... You'd never want to dispatch him with a rifle.... It's too easy to match ballistics!

Shall we take stock of the ways you can unwittingly intimidate the poor fool taking your daughter out? There are the angles from which you communicate; the distance at which you stand relative to the message recipient; the posture you utilize (likely displaying ownership of your surroundings); your chin angle; the tone of your voice; even the arch of your eyebrows. All of these can deliver less-than-subtle indicators of displeasure.

There is another advantage to you beginning your relationship with the boyfriend by putting him at ease, and that is wiggle room down the road. At some point you may need to apply varying degrees of pressure, and if you've built great rapport, you'll have a friendly place to launch the psychological war games from. As Patrick Swayze said in *Road House*, "Be nice, until it's time to *not* be nice."

If your meeting is adversarial from the outset (in nonverbal terms) and things turn ugly during their later dating weeks, you'll have to increase your physical dominance displays to obnoxious levels to produce the same level of fear you could easily get in the first meeting. In other words, you're going to have to be a real asshole to make an impact on him if he already thinks of you as a temperamental and/or a constantly overprotective father. We are going to start off being nice, so the comparison to the fire-breathing dragon he might see later on has the impact we desire.

Alienating your daughter, lessening her trust of you, is another reason not to be too hard on Junior. If she feels like you've overstepped your boundaries, she might side with him down the road, regardless of what he did. You do not want to fight them both, so you're going to have to learn the art of being subtle. In the interest of always coming across as the dad intent on finding her the right guy, you must make her feel as if everything you do is in partnership with her, always keeping her feelings central to the mission. If you lose sight of this, you'll be cast aside faster than a pair of skid-marked tighty-whities.

More Nonverbal Signals

When he knocks on the door, don't step into the doorway to shake his hand. This effectively blocks the entrance to your home, immediately making him feel like an intruder. Step back and away, and turn your body slightly so that he can freely enter. Wait until he is inside before offering a firm, not bone-crushing, handshake. Ensure that your thumb is vertical to the floor. If your thumb is turned out and the palm is in an upward (supinated) position you'll infer servitude, and if your hand is palm down (pronated) you'll indicate your feeling of dominance, also not something you want to make obvious.

Raise your eyebrows subtly; this opens up the eyes and lets a person know you pose no threat and are at ease, even interested, in what you see. At the same time, deliver a medium-intensity smile. Everything you do will have to be practiced and smooth, with no hint of falsehood or pretention. It must be genuine if it is to be received in the correct manner.

It is important that your chin remain at a neutral height. You should neither raise your chin too high nor lower it too much, at least not yet. Chin height is important because displays that open up the throat indicate overconfidence and/or contempt. We only show our throats to those we are comfortable with and unafraid of. For example, the face is lifted when we are smiling because we are excited to see an old friend—or because we are in the company of someone we feel superior to and whom we know poses no physical threat. Although an old friend won't take it like this, a raised chin can give the impression of arrogance, as it results in our "looking down our nose" at the recipient. Alternatively, a horizontal chin position gives nothing away and warms the impact of a medium-sized smile. If you are shorter or taller than him, align your entire face with his. Don't just move your eyes. Misaligning your face, up or down, will provide subconscious clues that you aren't a fan of his.

If you smile too much, you'll be perceived as too friendly and this will make him suspicious. The last thing you want is him wondering why you're so happy to meet him. It may propel him down the path of thinking your daughter might be loony, and that you're in a hurry to marry her off.

Conversely, if you don't smile genuinely enough, the emotion engages only the lips, and excludes the eyes. You'll look like the shark in *Finding Nemo* and, once again, his guard will be up. A nice, happy medium is best. If there's any doubt in your mind about whether your smile is the perfect balance between pleasant and not too enthusiastic, ask your wife. She will be the first to tell you where your smile lands on the scale between friendly father and Hannibal Lecter.

Now, I'll need you to own it! When we meet someone for the first time and are not that eager for the introduction, we tend to shorten our verbal greeting and our eye contact. Or worse yet, we glare menacingly (eyebrows lower, chin lower, lips compressed together), as the inconvenience of it all makes us mad. Sometimes these signals are deliberate and well thought-out, but often they are displayed without conscious intent, if even for a fraction of a second, and immediately indicate we couldn't give a hoot about meeting that person whatsoever.

I was once greeted with contempt by the head honcho at a corporate event where I was the keynote speaker. He interacted with everyone, including me, with an arrogance that left me wanting to kick him in the stones. Given that I was there to enlighten his group with my presentation on more effectively reading body language, one would think he'd have tried to at least fake wanting to meet me, but he didn't. He was so accustomed to being the top dog within his organization that it no longer occurred to him that outside his normal bubble, people might take issue with his behavior—something I immediately did.

As is often the case when I present at large corporate gatherings, I had arrived at this event early enough to observe as much of the "goings on" as possible. I rarely miss this intelligence-gathering opportunity. It allows me to see firsthand how everyone from executives to salespeople interact with one another and what morale is like.

I always allow for some uncomfortable jitters when I meet folks for the first time. Even those who have booked me for the purpose of presenting on the topic of interpreting body language sometimes aren't sure what to do with their hands, or whether I can tell they might be a little nervous interacting with me. In these cases, I usually go out of my way to be as warm and fuzzy as possible, and put their minds (and hands) at ease. But I couldn't bring myself to be warm to this boss. In fact, being the stroppy S.O.B. that I sometimes am, I decided to mess with him.

During his greetings with members of his group, I noticed he had a tendency to pat people on the shoulder, much like one might pat a dog. Worse still, he would be looking around the room for the next person to approach before the individual was through saying hello. In addition, his feet would be more widely spaced than necessary for good balance or posture (a territorial display), and he would deliver his greeting with his chin slightly raised, helping to ensure everyone understood who was in charge.

I had the opportunity to watch him for several minutes before he approached with the exact amount of genuine enthusiasm (next to none) I expected. I wanted to have fun with him, and as soon as he moved into the ready position to present his handshake, I knew what to do. As was customary, he went to a high-arm, palm-down position, something that generates more height. Like spreading the feet too wide, magnifying height delivers the same message: I believe myself to be dominant over you. A small caveat should be mentioned at this time: I also meet people at these events who are genuinely excited to meet me. Those individuals also have a tendency to go high-arm swinging prior to the handshake, but their other nonverbal signals are not arrogance displays, they are excitement ones. And when we are genuinely excited or happy, we tend to be a bit more jaunty in our step and more erect in our posture. As soon as our hands touched, I turned his hand into a palm-up position while interrupting the verbal delivery of his title within the company. I interrupted him by saying, "Don't pat me." This threw him off his well-rehearsed, pompous delivery of his title. His patting hand had already begun its journey toward my shoulder and immediately froze in midair. I kept a firm grip of his hand, now trapped within my two hands, so I could control the speed and pace of the shake as I explained why I didn't want him to pat me. "I have a very unusual rash on that shoulder that's been itching for weeks. Contact of any sort makes it flare up, and right before I go up to present that can be terrible. I'm sure you understand." He understood very well. I know he did because his superior expression became one of horror as he tried in vain to retract his hand from beneath mine. I didn't release. Instead, I pretended to be oblivious to his attempted pullback, as I asked where I should go to set up for my presentation. I didn't release his hand until I was sure I'd made him so uncomfortable that I wouldn't have to deal with him approaching me again.

A case this bad doesn't happen very often. I share it with you to illustrate my point that feeling superior to others can prime your behavior to project in a particular way. A shift in perspective can manifest positive, nonverbal signals where there were once horrendous superiority indicators. Not changing your thinking can leave you vulnerable to contracting nasty rashes from people who won't let go of your hand until they've shared them with you.

If you tell yourself before the initial meeting that you are not superior to your daughter's boyfriend, you'll physically emulate someone the boyfriend won't mind opening up to. It is all about your mind-set and attitude before you greet him.

Once you have warmly guided the boyfriend into the kitchen (one of the most socially acceptable rooms to hang out in), you may begin asking easy, nonthreatening questions, but not before letting him know how long it will be before your daughter is ready to come down and reveal herself for the date. Another reason for you and your daughter to be on the same page in regard to you getting a chance to meet the boyfriend is her understanding that you can't possibly learn what you need to learn if he's in your company for only a few minutes. It's also your choice as to whether your wife joins you for the chat. There are pros and cons to either arrangement. If your wife is there, he might feel as if he is under too much scrutiny, especially as it dawns on him that there are going to be more than the normal amount of social questions. This pressure could equate to changed normal behavior, or it could have the opposite effect, making him feel more comfortable with the additional protection (or at least a witness) to ensure things aren't too intense. I think this depends on you, your wife, and what makes you, the interviewer, more relaxed.

He must be accessible to you for at least ten minutes before your daughter joins the conversation or says she's ready to go. You should let him know this ballpark time when he comes in. This should not be so long that it causes added panic on his part, nor so much time that uncomfortable silences creep in; it should simply be long enough for you to get a feel for who he is.

If you don't provide him with a ballpark time for her to be down, he will display nonverbal signals of being nervous about how long your time together might be. Once more, we want him at ease in the knowledge that whatever you are about to discuss won't go longer than ten minutes. He will think he can handle anything for that time period, and since you will be nice, he should be able to. In addition, you won't have to worry yourself with discerning whether his body language signals are a result of his being preoccupied with when the lady of the hour shall appear. This exchange is also a chance for you to make a small joke about women always needing more time to get ready than men, or something along these lines that isn't demeaning to your daughter, but encourages a sense of camaraderie between the two of you, a couple of regular guys.

In general terms, when a person, male or female, feels threatened, stressed, or defensive, it is not unusual for them to limit how many hand gestures they use while talking. This lack of hand mobility (also called illustrators) communicates a great deal about the mental state of the person. In the following chapter, we will address how and why this is important when you are reading the "subject," but for now this information is important because your own lack of gestures during a meeting will speak volumes about your mind-set.

We also have a tendency to restrict arm and hand movements when we are poised to attack. I'm not sure if you will feel inclined to attack your daughter's boyfriend, but in case you do, be aware that when you stop using hand motions during communication, you become more menacing.

During caveman days (and also today if you hunt), there was a need for people to creep up on a food source or a fellow caveman without alerting them. Movement, justifiably, became limited and slow; the last thing you'd do during a stalk is start waving your arms around. Chatting with the new boyfriend, especially when you are reading him and concentrating on what he is saying, can bring out the same response. Thinking hard, much like concentrating on stalking an animal, inhibits natural movements. As fathers we naturally want to be threatening. We are, after all, protecting what is most precious to us, so who wouldn't have an urge to be a little scary—but Kato, now is not the time.

We tend to become a little clumsy, and wooden, if we overthink things. So for a few weeks before you meet the boyfriend, be aware of what type and size of hand gestures you typically use while talking with family and friends. You'll find you have go-to hand gestures, usually influenced by the topic of conversation and the emotion experienced during the discussion. We often use our hands to show scale or illustrate a particular point. The hands support what we say and move with the ebb and flow of our words. When you begin focusing your attention on what someone else is telling you, both verbally and nonverbally, they can halt. Then the cognitive load, the amount of work our brains are required to endure while watching and listening to every nuance of communication displayed, is too much. One can't naturally coordinate hand movements while also managing all that thinking—this takes practice.

This practice is a little like walking. You walk every day with little to no problems, until you are asked to go onstage in front of a room full of people. Suddenly walking requires immense focus so you don't screw it up by tripping and making an idiot of yourself. The additional thinking calls on different parts of the brain to "help" with the task of walking to the center of the stage. That extra brain function interferes with the muscles that have been doing the job for years, and now you have basically self-sabotaged—and a fall is much more likely. It takes practice to perform natural movements when the emotions you are experiencing are at odds with what you want, or need to display.

Even your blink rate may decline as you stare at your target and pick apart every twitch. Sadly for him, he will, accordingly, find himself twitching more than he should, as you have come to resemble a human mannequin with a thousand-yard stare, with your arms hanging stiffly by your sides or crossed in front of your chest, not moving at all. You will resemble a guy poised to commit violence, not host a friendly chat. Both of these positions look completely unnatural; and although the arms crossed is a staple position for men the world over, the recipient will still wonder just how far up your ass the stick must actually go. Your arms and hands must do what your arms and hands usually do, flow and move in time with your words and conversation.

Don't begin idle chat until you are standing in a position to observe all of his responses. Any questions asked when you can't observe his signals are wasted opportunities. He may chat and ask you questions as you lead him into your home, and it's fine to respond. If he doesn't, it's okay to fill dead-air time with idle chatter. Just don't ask any of your baseline or important questions until you are in the kitchen. (Note: Idle chatter on your part is a good thing, as one of the most uncomfortable experiences between folks who've just met is silence. There is a time and place to use quiet as an effective interview tool, but this particular time isn't it.) Answer his questions or fill the short time walking to your destination with an interesting anecdote and/or lighthearted banter. He will be subconsciously sizing you up as you walk, taking stock of things like your gait, how broad your back is, if you walk like a man who knows what he's doing in a fight, and most of it is involuntary and primal.... The more you chat, the less time there is for him to consciously analyze what's he's seeing.

Once you are in the kitchen, find an unobstructed position to observe him and angle your body slightly away from his. Do not square off, facing him fully. Ventral orientation (the direction your belly button faces) during a conversation affects one's ability to build rapport. Men interact with one another more comfortably when they are at slight angles from each other. They orient their trunks toward neutral ground if the exchange is nonconfrontational. Conversely, the opposite is normally true for women. Women typically feel more comfortable facing one another, as this allows them to fully commit their attention to the exchange. They engage not just their ears, but their whole bodies, to immerse themselves in the conversation. Women communicate more effectively than men because of this.

We men fear attack from the front (women from behind), and standing facing a male conversation partner can instantly increase tension, unless the guys are good friends and there is complete trust between them. (FYI: The new boyfriend doesn't trust you yet and that's okay, as you don't trust him either.)

Creating an offset by directing your trunk into the room and not toward the young man will afford you more nonverbal ammunition down the road. When the time comes to increase the pressure and scare him a tad, ventral orientation will play a major role. This is a trick you'll want in your tool bag.

You are now positioned perfectly (figuratively and literally) to begin asking low-impact questions and observe his responses. Take measure of the lad and you'll be able to compare aspects of how he answers the "easy" stuff with the upcoming tougher questions. But before we make that jump, you need to keep him talking, and the easiest and yet most often overlooked aspects of keeping a person chatting and feeling comfortable are eye contact and a nodding head. You don't need to resemble one of those bobblehead dolls, just nod slightly as he talks and look interested. If he's telling you something slightly funny, maintain a slight smile, at least with your eyes. If he is sharing something interesting, lift your eyebrows slightly to encourage him to share more, and keep your little nod going. If the topic changes to something moving, stop smiling and look moved, but keep your subtle head affirmations going. People really do love to talk about themselves and require only a little encouragement to keep them going. So encourage him. Be interested, inquisitive, warm, and encouraging, and he'll probably talk your ears off!

It is your responsibility to develop quick rapport, and then use it to keep him opening up. His job is to make a quick but good impression, and then escape with your daughter in tow. It is the information gathered by you during this exchange that will help you decide what sort of bloke he is, but if he doesn't open up because you are glaring at him, you will have wasted the opportunity.

As you have a better idea now of ways to make yourself more receptive and likeable after you two guys meet, we need to get back to Junior and the first few seconds of appraising him, the ones that are often overlooked. The walk from his car to your house allows you a precious few seconds to scrutinize how he walks, the clothes he wears, even what he does with his hands as he approaches. I know this is a lot more scrutiny than you've ever wanted to commit to another guy, but no information when it comes to assessing someone is superfluous to note. It all means something, and in the next chapter, you'll learn how to use my appraisal guide to make an effective and accurate read of a person in three seconds or less. It is going to take practice, but once you have these guidelines down pat, you'll be able to maximize the following ten minutes with Junior, and ask questions based in part on what you have identified in your speed-read.

CHAPTER FOUR

The First Three Seconds

> "Man is the only animal that can remain on friendly terms with the victims he intends to eat until he eats them."
>
> —Samuel Butler

The above statement couldn't be more true. During my survival training to get into the Commandos, every man was issued a bunny to kill and eat after days without food. Unfortunately, due to bunny contraception, or British funding issues, there weren't quite enough rabbits to go around.

After spending most of my childhood in the countryside, killing and skinning a rabbit wasn't a big deal for me. At least not compared to its impact on the guys who came to training from the city and may never before have had an opportunity to dispatch, skin, and eat a meal of their own making. So I volunteered to be one of the guys to skip having a rabbit. I would still eat one; I just wouldn't actually kill the poor little bugger before I did. Well, this went down like a wet fart in church. The training team presumed that my lack of interest in dispatching Thumper was a result of me being squeamish, something that couldn't have been further from the truth—but arguing with the training cadre is pointless. They devised a plan to take the cutest bunny they could find from one of the other recruits and give it to me. They also insisted that I tie a pink ribbon in a bow around its neck and never put the animal down, or stop stroking it. (Yes, a special trip was made by a member of the training team to find a pink ribbon, as this is not standard Commando issue.) This was to be my punishment for a twenty-four-hour period, to test my resolve when the order was given to break its neck. Over the next twenty-four hours, the bunny and I became great friends as the training team came up with what they saw as funnier and funnier ways to make the two of us bond.

I was instructed to talk to the bunny. I had to take it for a walk on the end of the pink ribbon. I was told to whisper how much I loved it into its ears; massage its shoulders; rub its feet; and the grand finale, give it half a dozen French kisses. By this time, I'm sure the rabbit was beginning to think we were made for each other. I've never had a pet look so freaking relaxed. I could walk the animal around with him lying on his back in my arms like a newborn baby. Then the big morning arrived, and our time together was up. Everyone was gathered around to witness what they were sure was going to be me making a mess of dispatching the animal. At the very least, they expected some tears on my part; after all, the fluffy bunny had spent an entire twenty-four hours in my pocket, sometimes literally. With the training team's eyes and those of other potential Royal Marine Commandos boring into me, the snickering began. I stepped into the middle of the circle of men, stroking the ears of my new furry best friend, and then just as I'd practiced every time the training team hadn't been watching over the previous twenty-four hours, I hung him upside down by his rear feet. He had become so used to this little routine that he didn't even wriggle. He just hung there, happy, passive, and relaxed. And then, very quickly, I struck the back of his neck with the edge of my hand in one swift, violent movement, cleanly breaking the neck. He twitched a couple of times, and that was it. He was gone. The training team looked shocked and one of them muttered, "Damn, that was cold...."

Interest quickly vanished in watching me skin him since I wasn't upset by the process. I've always thought this was all a little strange, as it happened during a training program that taught, "Be nice. Be respectful to all people." (But it also taught us to keep in the back of our mind that we might have to kill them one day.) In hindsight, I know that the lesson was to teach a certain detachment from those you might have to deal with. Because if shit ever hits the fan, you might have to follow orders and take them out.

When the time comes for you to interact with the boyfriend, I would like you to focus on the "act" portion of interact. You need to seem present, personable, compassionate, and real. But also in your mind, you are watching his dance with detached curiosity, because one day he might do something you don't agree with and you'll need to hang him by his ankles.

When we think about nonverbal signals, we typically think about crossed arms or eye rolling, or some other obvious body language signals. But there is so much more to taking stock of someone. Long before a person begins communicating verbally, he has told you many things about himself that can escape scrutiny if you aren't paying attention. The following list of things to look for is something I share with the attendees of my events right before calling people up onstage to meet me. There's nothing better than going through each of the items below, one at a time, giving examples of what to look for, and then asking someone to walk through the crowded room for all to see. It adds the kind of pressure and anxiety your daughter's boyfriend should be feeling before he meets you and Mom.

Often, before my presentations, I make a point of pacing the front of the room. This isn't because I'm nervous. I do it because it allows me to claim the space as mine as early in the presentation as possible. Without even realizing it, attendees who might otherwise utilize the front of the room to find available seating, now go out of their way to avoid walking into that area at all. Occasionally, however, someone will go straight through the middle, regardless of how many times I've paced across the area. That person will always be my first target to be called out and have their body language read in front of the group. If you're cocky enough to feel entitled to share the stage, you should be cocky enough to handle being scrutinized in front of the seminar attendees.

Have a quick gander at the following list:

- Space
- Gait
- Posture
- Stance
- Gestures
- Facial expressions
- Words
- Tone
- Volume
- Cadence
- Clothing
- Accessories
- Smell

If I asked you right now to check off these items the next time you meet someone, you'd probably be a smidge overwhelmed. Those are a lot of things to remember all at once. One of the most challenging aspects of trying to assess all of these during a first meeting is that it causes us to use up valuable cognitive horsepower that would otherwise be dedicated to us being concerned about how we are coming across. I don't know about you, but I'm already challenged enough in the cognitive department and the last thing I need is to add extraneous items to think about. So I'm happy to announce some good news: you don't have to worry about how you are coming across to the wee lad, as you will have practiced all of the aforementioned rapport-building skills to ensure you come across as a reasonably nice guy. As long as you are able to create rapport and put the boy at ease, you've achieved one of your key goals.

You don't have to be overly concerned with how he perceives you, at least not in the way you may be with others. Smile, be nice, and cross excessive worrying about your facade off your list of subjects to think about. You're going to need every ounce of horsepower to read the young man loitering in your kitchen. And how he loiters will tell you a lot about his personality.

When it comes to the utilization of your space during the meeting, it's similar to my claiming the front of the auditorium prior to presenting. He is in your domain and shouldn't lay claim to owning any territory. Let's say you invite him into your home and he immediately heads to a particular spot in the kitchen and lounges against the countertop. There are two possible reasons for this. He could be a cocky S.O.B. and feel entitled to claim ownership over whatever space he wants, or, and this'll sting, he's been in the kitchen before and already feels perfectly at ease there. The latter of these problems (if no one informed you of his previous visit) will need to be addressed with your daughter on your own time. I don't want to get anywhere near that one. For now I'm interested in the first reason.

Claiming ownership over a space is done by people who either are full of themselves or are trying to show false bravado and give the appearance of indifference. Oftentimes, guilty perps will lounge back in their chairs during police interviews in the hopes of giving the appearance of a carefree, guilt-free impression. It says, "I'm not bothered by your questions, you've got nothing on me, and if I was guilty I'd never look this relaxed." Well, we know the difference. Claiming surface area in your kitchen by lounging is supposed to give you the same impression—and in case you haven't caught on yet, this is a problem. We would prefer someone relaxed, but still upright. Comatose over your countertop is not a good sign.

Another unfavorable display would be a wide foot stance, also taking up space and utilizing real estate. Foot spacing wider than shoulder width will look theatrical. In evolutionary terms, spreading the legs allows the "junk" to hang freely. In addition to claiming more space, it is a less-than-subtle announcement that he thinks his are bigger than yours and he doesn't feel a need to protect them from you. It tells us a lot about how he perceives himself, and in life, self-perception is everything. How we would like to be seen by others influences nearly everything we do. In this wide-stance example, he wants to be recognized as dominant and powerful, and those projections nearly always originate from fear. Anyone, but particularly a man (or boy), who is motivated by fear can be erratic, emotional, controlling, and prone to temper tantrums when he doesn't get his way. Spatial, territorial displays that seem over the top provide nearly instant insight into his attitude and character, and let you know very early in the meeting what sort of a person you are dealing with. However, he might also do things right. And by right, I mean he exhibits behavior displays representative of a young man intent on making a good impression because he's a nice guy.

Perhaps the young man follows you dutifully into the kitchen and for a few moments doesn't know where to stand. He will look a little lost, possibly like a deer in the headlights, and end up standing stock-still, not moving anywhere. He might not blade his body away from you, something that under normal (interaction with a contemporary) circumstances might happen within a few seconds, and instead orients toward you, with normal to narrow foot spacing and hands down by his sides. Take note of the lack of movement here. It means that he probably isn't taking time to review the new environment because the only thing that is a potential threat to his health right now is you. On any other day, he would take inventory of his surroundings. Today, you are all he is focusing on, and that concern takes up such a large part of his thinking, that normal behavior comes in at a distant second place. How he is using the space he resides in at this moment is perfectly normal. Actually, he is likely being a tad too fearful, so you may need to make extra effort to put him at ease. Too much anxiety, just like too much cockiness, is a bad thing. We'd like a happy medium. You don't want him claiming large amounts of space by lounging, but also don't want him standing at perfect attention either. One can lean, relax, and use support without lounging, and this would be a happy medium. If he does look around during the short time it takes to find a spot to stand, and he does it moving his head rather than with furtive eyeball movements, it shows an appropriate measure of calm and confidence, something we want him to have.

Then there is his gait. John Wayne, Clint Eastwood, Charles Bronson, Gerard Butler in *300*, even Keanu Reeves as Neo in *The Matrix* had memorable gaits. They each had a particular way of walking, and I'm betting with just a few minutes' consideration, you'll find the common thread—and no, it's not weird that a bunch of straight dads are now spending a few minutes thinking about the on-screen swagger inherent in those actors' movements. Well, it's a little bit strange, but I'm confident in my machismo and I hope you are, too! And it's for a very good cause. If you are able to observe the boyfriend as he walks around your home, or after exiting his vehicle (or the taxi he's using due to a license suspension), you'll gain more insight into his personality. Personally, I'd be extremely displeased to see a John Wayne–type swagger while making his way to my front door. It looks great in movies, but not so great in reality. I know it's too much to ask for a nervous Edward Scissorhand (minus the scissors) to shuffle his way down my driveway, but you get my point: many things are revealed by the way a person walks. And swaggering, unless you've spent the last three days riding a pony in the Himalayas, is a warning sign of things to come.

Teenage boys *especially* shouldn't swagger. They haven't experienced enough life outside of high school to earn a swagger. If they are already doing it, then they probably presume themselves to be a large fish in, what you and I know is, a small pond. As you can imagine, ego plays a large part in this front and is always something to be managed carefully. At this juncture, if you are aware that you are dealing with an overinflated sense of self, you can use this to your advantage and subtly flatter your way to an initial good rapport. What we'd like to see are normal-paced steps, a moderate arm swing, relaxed shoulders, and the impression that he isn't trying too hard.

We've now looked at his potential stance, the way he might use or take up space, and his potential gait. Posture is different than stance, but I often lump them together when I'm quickly observing someone. I think of them as fluid, changing regularly depending on circumstances. For instance, stance, particularly as it relates to the position of one's feet, can change during an interaction due to physical comfort. No one likes to stand in the exact same position for an extended period. But it can also change because the topic of conversation has suddenly become uncomfortable. The stance may narrow as a feeling of vulnerability occurs—and in men this often relates to a subconscious feeling that one's groin needs protecting. A sudden onset of foot tapping can indicate excitement, or a desire to escape a situation. Context will dictate which is most likely based on when the action occurred. The feet are always of interest because they are so far away from the brain and as such are often forgotten and not controlled as well as the upper body might be. With this said, posture tends to fluctuate more than stance, and I find myself paying more attention to it once a conversation begins. You can always use peripheral vision to keep track of the feet, as those movements tend to be larger and thus more noticeable.

Think of a postural change as something that occurs from the waist up. It can be impacted by mood or attitude, temperature change, or conversation. Both the verbal exchange with a person and the internal dialogue that occurs in our minds as a conversation unfolds.

One of the things that makes reading someone's body language changes difficult is that they can result from an internal thought unrelated to the verbal conversation. If something catches your eye, including a postural change, and you immediately think, "Ha! I gotcha," consider that all you are seeing is a signal that may or may not be an emotional response to your questions. It could be a result of a conversation going on in his head, not the one you are a part of. But if you observe an immediate, questionable reaction to your verbal conversation, then you'll need to probe the matter further. Consider bringing it up again later and seeing if the reaction happens again. Until you have confirmation that your read was accurate, all you've got is a nonverbal signal to take note of—nothing more. Generally speaking, though, posture that lifts or expands the body indicates a positive response (unless you are arguing, in which case it indicates aggression!); whereas slumping, shrinking, covering oneself with one's arms, or withdrawing all have negative, or insecure, emotional associations.

For those of you who have had the opportunity to sit through an English soccer match, you may have noticed the stance and posture opposing competitors assume when there's a free kick coming their way. For those of you who haven't, I shall describe it: a wall of three or four players line up in front of the guy awarded the free kick on the opposite team. They are there to provide a barrier of meat between the kicker and their goalpost, making scoring a point off the kick difficult. As a rugby bloke myself, I couldn't really give a hoot about soccer or free kicks, but what interests me is the position that the players assume in defense of the free kick. Their hands drop and clasp in front of their family jewels to protect the sensitive area from potential impact after the leather projectile is kicked in their direction.

The players may never have had a soccer ball smack them in the nuts, but they'll swiftly cover those puppies up when there is a chance it could happen, and I don't blame them. Covering and protecting our most precious area when we feel threatened or vulnerable is something we men are prone to do. If, as previously considered, Junior covers his groin with his hands during your conversation, and you aren't threatening to physically kick him in his nether regions, then he is likely experiencing a feeling of vulnerability. Be aware that someone who feels vulnerable may also or instead use furniture or other inanimate objects as a cover. Your kitchen island might serve perfectly as a protective barrier, as would a chair. If Junior changes locations to use such an object as a barrier, read this the same as you would if he was covering his groin with his hands.

Covering one's stomach, whether it's with the arms, the furniture, or even a cup of tea pulled close to the body, is done for the same reasons as a groin cover. The throat, one of the most vulnerable areas on the body, will rarely be covered by a man, but is often covered by a woman. Men rub the back of their neck in times of stress to self-soothe; women sometimes do this, too, but they will also place a hand to the front of their neck to protect the area. This speaks volumes about the male psyche. Covering the groin is a must; but blocking a blow to the neck, which could be life threatening, isn't considered.

Women are most likely to cover their throats when they feel scared or trapped, something you might want to keep in mind the next time you ask your daughter where she's been for the last few hours. If the young man in your kitchen appears to feel vulnerable and you haven't begun your interview, then it is up to you to try to get him to relax. If he suddenly performs a groin-protection move or hides behind obstacles because you are asking him prying questions, then continue doing so! You've obviously hit a nerve, now find out which one.

But what if his hands never cover his nether regions or stomach? Let's say he strolls into your kitchen, stops at his location of choice, and places both hands on his hips? And no, that doesn't mean you can run up and kick him in the balls. Not yet, at least. It means that he reacted to you (or your questions) in a way that made him feel the need to make himself appear larger and better able to defend himself. A hands-on-hips posture makes the upper body look larger and shows you're ready to use your elbows as self-defense, in necessary. Arms that swing from front to back and result in hands that slap together achieves a similar effect. The contact can be gentle or firm, but the meaning is the same—he is claiming more space and showcasing his "weapons," his hands. These movements are nearly always subconscious, and they're one you often see when you watch small guys chat with large ones. If you frequent the gym, you'll see a lot of this (in addition to all the peacocking and strutting that goes on in front of mirrors). The smaller of the two begins a sort of dance to use up space and showcase his willingness to defend if the need arises. You will rarely see the larger male doing this, unless the shorter bloke happens to be a dangerous fellow. Then, if the perception by the larger male is that he might be in jeopardy, he might assume a position or motion that takes up more space or shows off his "guns" more effectively.

Many years ago, I knew a guy at my local gym who would place his foot on equipment in an elevated position when he chatted with people, male or female. His stance was supposed to yell, "I have no need to defend or protect my tenders from you, as I don't perceive you as a threat." What level of arrogance does that show? As, for a short time, I was his Muay Thai kickboxing instructor, he didn't have the audacity to do this when we talked, and certainly not when we trained. I found this interesting because it showed he wasn't making the displays in front of others as a conscious decision—they were merely a result of how he perceived himself. He considered himself invulnerable.

Postures and stances that promote size or insinuate a feeling of invulnerability are indicative of an underlying lack of confidence or extreme overconfidence. Depending on what other signals are also manifesting with the boyfriend, you might need to fine-tune your tactics during the initial preamble and opening questions salvo. Chances are that if the boyfriend uses a pompous posture in your kitchen, it could be his way of trying to measure up to you. But if you don't have your own insecurities, you won't try matching him, and make the situation worse. This is not the time to mirror his body language—or list your manly accomplishments. It's the time to make nice and figure out who the hell your daughter is dating.

Of course, there's always a chance that he really is that arrogant, but you'll figure this out only by carefully watching him over the next ten minutes. During this time, you'll observe any warning signs displayed, to either validate or negate your initial assumptions.

Hand, arm, shoulder, head, and full-body movements can go along with or contradict the spoken word. Because we'll be covering these in more detail in the next chapter, I don't want to spend a great deal of time here on them. However, during the first few seconds of observing and meeting the current flavor of the month, you should pay special attention to how his arms and hands are utilized. Does he swing them enthusiastically as he makes his way down the driveway, or are they stiff and out of sync? If the arms are rigid this could indicate he is nervous (so long as that isn't the way he walks all the time). If the arms are like that, look at the hands: Are they balled into fists or squeezed more tightly than you would expect? Does he stuff his hands into his pockets as if he is trying to hide them? A by-product of stuffing one's hands into pockets, particularly jeans pockets, can push the shoulders up toward the ears, helping to retract the head. This head-retracted position is known as turtling up and indicates the person wants to literally keep a low profile. This could also be a sign of nerves or anxiety.

Alternatively, hands stuffed into pockets might be his go-to position, as a way to be comfortable, and then it doesn't mean anything. In this case, the shoulders will probably be relaxed, and the hands will come back into play during his time talking with you. For most people, it's hard to communicate without using the hands in some capacity. When I'm chatting, it looks like I'm trying to take flight, my hands move that much. Most people fall short of that amount of hand flapping; but for most, some hand motion is perfectly normal. As extended interactions fall outside the purview of our first few seconds of assessment time, just pay attention to where the hands are and what they do as he exits the vehicle and heads toward the front door. Then compare that to what he does with his hands once he is in your kitchen. We are interested in differences or changes in behaviors when he is in front of you, versus the walk to your house when he thinks you aren't watching. These changes can indicate shifts in attitude or emotions, and we are always interested in nonverbal indicators of internal emotional manifestations.

Facial expressions can be a doozy to begin reading. It's a skill that's hard to practice with family and friends, and still keep on their good side. Family is stuck with you, but that doesn't mean they won't start hiding their faces behind pillows or other household items, like pointed shotguns, when they realize you are studying them again. My recommendation is for you to go to http://www.paulekman.com and http://www.humintell.com and begin your facial-reading practice there. This will require you to part with a little of your hard-earned cash—but it isn't that much. (Note: I have no affiliation with the sources recommended in this book, except the Dad's Club website. I just think they're awesome and use them myself.)

I've had my kids sit with me while I practiced reading facial expressions, and it actually made learning with them fun. Of course, sharing this has had its drawbacks, too. They paid *very* close attention and became quite proficient at picking up on small changes on my face. This has proved both beneficial and a pain in the ass. The upside is that when I'm getting frustrated with them, they know from my expression to stop doing whatever it is that's driving me nuts. On the other hand, they also know when I'm not really mad and just being parental—and my son, especially, takes advantage of this. Everything has its ups and downs.

One of the first things I realized as I began my journey into reading facial expressions is how fast emotions can pass across a person's face. This is why it's so important to have a place to go to learn and practice your skills. Just being told what to look for would never do justice to how difficult it is to actually spot the subtle or fleeting micro-expressions that deliver a glimpse into the true emotions experienced by the subject. With speeds as long as half a second, and as short as 1/25 of a second, to just say they are "quick" would be like commenting that Usain Bolt is an okay runner who suffers from minor showboating issues.

Neither comment would do justice to his speed and ego. And then things get complicated because most people don't feel one emotion at a time. Invariably they are a mix of at least two emotions, and display accordingly. All of this will cause you trouble if you don't give yourself a chance to practice.

Paul Ekman, a professor of psychology at the University of California, San Francisco, has been researching facial expressions, body language, and human behavior for more than thirty years. We can thank him and his team for scientifically validating the observations made by Charles Darwin more than one hundred years before: that there are seven universal emotional expressions that cross virtually all cultural lines (although there are some cultural differences between when they are displayed):

1. Anger
2. Fear
3. Surprise
4. Sadness
5. Happiness
6. Contempt
7. Disgust

So, good news: if your daughter brings home a bloke from Outer Mongolia, you can still look for the same basic facial expressions that you would for a boyfriend from down the road. How cool is that? Come on, find that silver lining....

As there is no way to predict which one of the seven expressions might be displayed during your time with her boyfriend, I recommend you become proficient in reading them all. Especially because he may display a combination of them and you'll want to know what the blend comprises.

The one that will be of most interest is contempt. He might display this emotion for a variety of reasons, and none of them are good. Before we cover a few of those reasons, you need to know that contempt is disdain, dislike, and disrespect, and not necessarily in that order. If he showcases any of these within the first few seconds of your meeting him, and you've been playing nice to begin the rapport-building process, skip everything else and go straight to using a Taser on him. If you are unsure about where to acquire a good one (and the most painful areas of the body on which to use it), e-mail me. I'll send you an anonymous guidebook so you can familiarize yourself with some specifics.

If he shows contempt, I also suggest that you and your daughter have a long sit-down chat and decide where she's going to be living in the near future—because if she's into this kind of bloke, you've got nothing but major trouble coming down the road. The last thing you'll want to be doing is paying for her food and lodging if she hates you enough to begin inviting that kind of schmuck into your home. Of course, it might be worth checking that she isn't just pulling your leg before you begin packing her bags. Maybe she has a wicked sense of humor and is paying you back for all of those times you weren't sympathetic to her ails as a young lady. In this case, suck it up and take the joke like a man, and then breathe a huge sigh of relief. I have a friend whose twenty-two-year-old daughter is currently dating a white supremacist recently paroled from prison. And no, I'm not joking. The boyfriend has the Nazi ink and everything. Whenever my mate talks about her, he shakes his head in complete disbelief and macro-expresses pronounced sadness—and I can understand why.

Now, it's possible that you will observe contempt later on in your conversation, but the reasons for this will probably differ from why you might see it in the first few seconds. If he flashes contempt before you've even started asking questions, then he is most likely experiencing feelings of superiority based on his assumptions or observations about you. However, if after your initial meet and greet, he suddenly flashes contempt, think carefully about what you or he may have been saying right before this display. It could indicate that he thinks the question you just asked is stupid or beneath him, or if he has just finished talking, he could have told you a half-truth, or a flat-out lie. The resulting emotion has him feeling smug contempt about pulling one over on you. But just because you may be giving the impression that you believe every word that comes out of his mouth, doesn't mean you actually do. If he is feeling smug about spinning you a tall tale, rest assured the feeling will dissipate quickly. As soon as you start asking him to expand on the details of his story, he will realize that he is the one being duped, and it's his own words that are getting him into a pickle.

We will cover the face in more detail in Chapter Six, and we will cover words, tone, and cadence in Chapter Eight. But for the first few seconds of you two hanging out, volume, like facial expressions and physical presence, can aid initial readings. In fact, volume can be exploited as an extension of spatial dominance. You may have to go back a few years, but dig into those memory banks and recall the last time you attended a party where you didn't know many, if any, people there. Do you remember how attuned you were to those around you? For most people, going into a social setting like this is one of the most unsettling circumstances we can put ourselves through. That stress tends to make us hyperaware of the goings-on around us, especially the antics of those who are being loud.

I have never attended such a function and not spent the first thirty minutes standing with my back to a wall, observing the people around me. It's a habit that used to drive my wife nuts. Now she has come over to the dark side and stands there with me, also observing the hell out of people.

My wife and I have never liked people who try dominating a space through volume or stance, and it never takes long to identify them. They blast the airwaves with every exploit they have ever undergone, embellishing fact after fact until you start wondering what they are compensating for. I am always drawn to the folks standing around the perimeter of a room, also observing and taking their time in coming forward to introduce themselves. I've found that they are usually infinitely more interesting in the long run. If it turns out that they aren't, their quieter demeanor is significantly easier on the ears when they share the latest and greatest baseball stats, or their favorite knitting pattern.

Those who wield volume like a weapon, overwhelming everyone around them, should be ignored in a social setting, as they rarely have anything of real interest to share. If the young man you've invited into your home is much louder than necessary during the first few seconds of the encounter, and he doesn't have a medical issue impairing his hearing, you'd do well to interpret his volume in the same way you'd categorize a wide stance and oversized arm movements: cocky, arrogant, and with an overblown sense of his own self-importance. There really isn't any reason to be loud in your kitchen, unless you are mixing with a blender when he arrives and he's competing for your attention. Performing an activity other than reading him is not something I recommend; multitasking when you should be decoding someone limits your ability to do so. I know we all like to think we can multitask like a housewife on crack, but accepting limitations falls into the category of "earned wisdom." Of course, if Junior is yelling at you, this multitasking won't even be an option. You'll have a hard time *not* focusing on the verbal part of his communication.

Increased volume is a way to overshadow and distract a listener from the things the screamer doesn't want the conversation partner to focus on. If this happens, it becomes even more important to focus on what's displayed nonverbally. The person might not display arrogance signals other than the increased volume, and is simply getting carried away with his nerves or excitement. The latter emotion is of much greater concern to us dads because unless you happen to be a sports star or a rock star, there's little about meeting you that's exciting—sorry. He's there for the girl and the prospects of what may lie ahead, literally.

Clothing is like a costume. It aids us in presenting ourselves the way we want to be perceived. Social psychologists refer to this as Impression Management, and it gets this esteemed title because how we choose to dress runs deeper than just a thought about how to cover up. Once upon a time, clothing was merely a way to provide warmth so we could stay alive, survive the elements, and not embarrass ourselves on cold days, when shrinkage is an issue. Not so these days. The survival portion, not the shrinkage—that will always be an issue. We have access to a multitude of clothing choices and we choose what to wear based in great part on how we think of ourselves, and how we want to display that identity. Sometimes we choose clothing to promote who we think we are, and sometimes we choose clothing as a barrier to cover who we really are. And as if that isn't complicated enough, we also make clothing decisions based on our profession, social environment, and, occasionally, obligations. Meeting you is an obligation for your daughter's boyfriend, and one that is easily manipulated to conform to expectations. For instance, the boyfriend might prefer to wear leather pants and a string vest in his own time, but he knows he should dress differently with you to promote the right impression; so he shows up sporting a three-piece suit, ready to impress you.

A fellow Brit over here in the States recently recalled how a prospective suitor for his daughter came to his door, ready for their date, wearing skintight ripped jeans and hobnailed boots. He had pierced everything, and rounded out his wardrobe with a Marilyn Manson T-shirt that had seen better days. Based on this, do you think we can draw conclusions about what his self-identity is? I'm going to go out on a limb and say anti-establishment, anti-conformist, and probably anti–Hepatitis C vaccinations. Everything about his costume screamed, "I don't care if you like me. I am who I am. Take it or leave it." My fellow Brit chose to leave it. With polite, but firm, instructions, Dad explained to the young man that if he wanted to take his daughter on a date, then he was going to have to come back looking less like Buffalo Bill from *Silence of the Lambs* and more like Charlie Brown from, well, you know, *Charlie Brown*. It worked. After a short, thirty-minute departure, the boyfriend returned wearing slacks, a button-down, and some much-too-small, ill-fitting loafers. Personally, I would have taken the first outfit, maybe minus a piercing or two, rather than request the second. Falsely representing oneself with an alternative costume is merely putting a Band-Aid over the real issue, which was this kid's desire to rebel. Making him go home and change before allowing him to take the daughter out was a missed opportunity to chat and interview the subject while he was cocooned inside his chosen facade. But I understand why the British dad did what he did—he had a preconceived idea about what sort of costume his daughter's boyfriend should wear. But if our perception of what sort of clothing the lad should wear is so ingrained that we demand he change into something else when it doesn't fit the model, then we have allowed ourselves to grow biased in assessing the new flame based on who we think she should be dating, and not on who she wants to date.

Having asked a few simple questions of your daughter beforehand, you should have a pretty good idea who's going to be coming to your door. It would be odd for some guy she barely knows to show up looking like that, and expect her to drop everything to go out with him. So put your bias aside, get digging into her mind-set, and figure out why she likes this kind of bloke. She's made a conscious choice to associate with him, and in public. It might be time for you to adorn yourself with nipple piercings and "HATE LOVE" knuckle tattoos if you want to stay connected to her during her dating years. It will also help show your youthful, rebellious side. Hey, you can be "down" with a cause, too, right?

My other issue with making presumptions based on clothing is that it increases the ease with which we allow people to pass under our radar when they conform to our ideas of what "normal" looks like. Less scrutiny is given to folks who fit a particular aesthetic mold because we assume that if they dress like us, they must *be* like us. Unfortunately, nothing could be further from the truth. Just because a boyfriend shows up epitomizing the harmless boy-next-door look, doesn't mean he isn't a raging sociopath. At least the Marilyn Manson

T-shirt wearer advertised his issues. The lad wearing slacks and a button-down shirt could have learned how to blend into normal society—meanwhile every cat and dog in a fifteen-mile radius has ended up a permanent addition in the guy's basement meat collage.

The boyfriend may have dressed a particular way to lull you into trusting him, and ensure a second bite at the apple, your daughter. In his mind, he may think there's no faster way to disarm a potential "mark" than by presenting someone who "belongs" in that environment. All said, I don't care what he shows up wearing. I'm going to assess him as if I already know he's wearing last week's roadkill for underwear, and take nothing I see at face value. I will scrutinize him just as enthusiastically if he's wearing normal attire as I would if he showed up wearing something less appealing to my sensibilities.

Note, however, that accessories can aid in the development of an intended impression. I often ask my audiences to review, assess, and attribute reasons to the accessories I wear for presentations. This requires me to be *completely honest* when I reveal why I wear things, otherwise nothing is learned. For instance, I perpetually wear a paracord bracelet. This is something that might prove incredibly useful if I find myself lost and alone in the woods and need to construct a temporary shelter. But within the relatively luxurious confines of a hotel conference room, it may be useless—except that it isn't. Its usefulness in supporting my desired impression is priceless. It suggests I have a military background or at least enjoy outdoor pursuits, without me having to say so. This implies I participate in manly hobbies and navigate life prepped and ready for any contingency. I pride myself on being ready, for what specifically I don't know, but that's the point—it advertises my mind-set. It also allows for me to easily bond with others who share similar interests. Just mention zombies and you should easily strike up an hour's worth of conversation. Hey, I warned you that I tend to be completely honest—otherwise the groups won't learn what I want them to learn.

Another thing some notice is the watch I wear, a high-end sports chronograph. I feel that, like shoes, the watch maketh the man, and sporting something that only a select few recognize makes me feel good. Last, but by no means least, I always carry a heavy-duty, sharp folding knife. Since my time in the military, I haven't been able to stand feeling defenseless or helpless, and not having a decent blade results in both emotions. I'm sure a psychologist would have a field day analyzing all of this information, but I already have a pretty good idea why I adorn myself the way I do. That insight came by way of my realization that when it came to figuring out others and their reasons for choosing clothing and accessories, there was no better place to launch my research than by studying my own choices. And if that consideration was to have value, I knew I'd have to be brutality honest about the motivations behind my choices. As for you, I recommend the same approach. Only you can really know why you wear what you wear, and how that promotes or distracts from the impression you want to deliver. It sometimes takes soul-searching and digging into the not-so-obvious reasons behind your choices, but if you think long and hard enough, you'll decode your decisions and have a better ability to decode others' choices.

What I concluded about myself is that because I felt helpless as a child, I will now do anything to ensure a feeling of independence and self-security. I don't want to rely on anyone else to provide me with that well-being. My choice of watch is connected to my having been dirt poor as a child, and having struggled with a lack of money for many years as an adult, especially in the military. An expensive watch reminds me that I am no longer in that place, and that I have value—something else I never felt as a child. My decision to make the watch a more select, low-key, and non-mass-produced item was my way of ensuring that the average person wouldn't realize the watch is fancy, or expensive. Unless related to teaching people how to read others, I prefer to keep this private.

So why did I share all that insight with you? To provide greater understanding that clothing and accessory choices are motivated by reasons beyond simple extravagance, poor taste, and eccentricities. There are reasons for everything. What we cloak ourselves in tells a story, and with a little consideration, potential reasons behind our choices can be decoded.

Let us now revisit the account of the young man who showed up festooned with piercings and ripped jeans at my fellow Brit's door. Consider why he dressed this way. My guess is the following reasons, either exclusive of one another or in combination:

1. He is rebelling against his parents, particularly his father.
2. He has, or had, social challenges when he was younger and didn't feel like he belonged or was accepted by his peers. This feeling could be because of a multitude of things, a lisp or stutter, a lack of athleticism or coordination, a learning disability, or an aesthetic shortcoming, and now he wants to "control" how people react to him.

Rebelling against one's father is one of the more easily recognizable issues behind a costume. Many of us felt the urge to rise up against the authoritarian figure we had to deal with growing up, and one's appearance was a way to do so. Similarly, physical issues can make a person defensive around new people or ones who used to make fun of him. If a person still has a lisp or stutter when he gets older, this might be a dead giveaway for why he acts the way he does.

Nothing draws attention away faster from what we want to hide, our perceived shortfalls, than the presence of things not socially accepted. If we are used to persecution because of traits beyond our control, then we want to control what draws criticism, and an attack on one's clothing or accessories is not nearly as personal as an attack on one's physical disability.

Making the young lad leave and change his appearance will result in his armor being removed. And if when he comes back, he seems uncomfortable during your meeting, there will be no way to know if it's because your questions are throwing him out of sorts, or it's a result of his discomfort in the clothing.

Even a lack of accessories can tell you things about a person. What if he showed up having voluntarily stripped himself of the things he usually wears for self-protection? He might have a tendency to fidget with rings or piercings to soothe himself during stressful encounters, and now he's without these. If someone wears things for a long period of time, and then they suddenly remove them, they might continually "revisit" the empty space with probing fingers. A number of guys showed up for Commando training sporting facial hair or long, flowing locks; and after they were removed under orders, they couldn't help but keep stroking and feeling around for what was missing. If you pay attention, you'll see signs of the missing item and will know to attribute this nervous behavior to that factor. Especially pale skin where a ring usually resides, and holes in the earlobes, eyebrows, nose, or lips all indicate he once went through, or continues to be going through, a rebellious stage. He's now either given up the need to continue the fight or taken them out five minutes before coming through your front door, as your daughter told him they wouldn't go down very well with her inside-the-box dad.

When, during my presentations, I talk about taking note of a person's smell, it always initiates a few titters. In fact, most people immediately begin thinking about some poor girl on a New York subway, squashed during rush hour and having her hair sniffed by some pervert standing closer to her than necessary. Don't laugh. I once had a female self-defense student who had experienced that during her time in a big city. Unfortunately, her sniffer had himself a quick grope, too. She had to abandon her ride home six stops earlier than she wanted, in order to escape the bastard.

Let's face it, my telling you to take a good long sniff of your daughter's boyfriend sounds pretty weird. But I don't mean that sort of creepy sniffing. I mean for you to grab a simple, well-camouflaged sniff as you shake his hand and welcome him into your home. Then, ask yourself these questions:

1. Does he smell clean or unwashed?
2. Is his aftershave application nauseatingly overpowering?
3. Is his breath minty? Is it too minty?
4. Does he smell like alcohol, cigarettes, cigars, or hash?
5. Does he have a diesel- or gasoline-engine-oil smell?
6. Does he smell like the ass end of a dead camel?
7. Can you detect the faint aroma of cats or dogs on him?

Most likely, all you're going to smell when you sniff him is an overabundance of cheap cologne or Old Spice deodorant stolen from his dad's bathroom cabinet. But not considering that he might smell like alcohol or weed would be a huge oversight. He could be drunk or high as a kite. A quick sniff could indicate intoxication, or mental impairment.

As for an aftershave overdose, this screams immaturity. Most of us outgrow bathing ourselves in a heavy-duty man fragrance about the same time our second nut drops. But a select few doggedly hold on to the notion that if a little makes him smell good, then pints must make him irresistible to women everywhere.

When I think of this level of immaturity, I think good news and bad news. The good news is that if he still thinks an abundance of cologne will make him more attractive to females, then he doesn't know women very well and is probably going to be a fumbling bag of nerves when it's time to go down to fondle town. The best thing that can happen here is he's so nervous that he doesn't want to make a move, especially a wrong move, and make an idiot of himself (more than the overpowering odor has already done)—and so will wait for her to do it for him. If your daughter decides that's okay and she does make the first move, then you're shit out of luck. Not much you can do about that, I'm afraid. But if she is a bit old-fashioned (because of all those great discussions she had with you about sex), then his nervous fumbling should kill the mood faster than having Dad sitting in the backseat with them.

The bad news is that immaturity can lead to temper tantrums, and her saying no to his pathetic advances could make the little bugger stroppy and prone to mood swings. Giving advance warning to your daughter about stroppy, immature guys and their potential danger is another must-do, alongside the chat covering narcissists. It could pay dividends down the road in terms of her recognizing the signs and steering herself clear of potential trouble.

If his breath is too minty, this could be a warning that he's trying to obscure something sinister like alcohol or weed consumption, or worse yet, planning on using his vernacular muscle for something other than chatting. Smells of smoke, cigarette or otherwise, are warning signs that he's a bit of a bad boy, or trying to use the habit to calm his nerves before meeting you. I think it's worth mentioning that for those of us who don't smoke, being around those who do is pretty nasty. Kissing the mouth of someone who smokes is like dragging your tongue around the bottom of a dirty old ashtray, and appeals about as much as a lobotomy. If your daughter is going out with this guy, she probably knows he smokes, and is likely doing that herself. This is the only way being around someone with the habit is remotely tolerable. You and I might not want to think our princess is the sort to be sucking on a cancer stick during her downtime, but this is a warning sign that she might be doing exactly that. It certainly warrants further investigation.

What if he shows up with the faint smell of gasoline or diesel oil? This might actually be a good sign. Most of what we are looking for is inherently negative. As dads, it is our responsibility to err on the side of looking for the worst, and then figure out how bad things really are, so we can formulate a plan of defense. But a young man who works on his own car or truck, or has a part-time job fixing other people's vehicles, is showing initiative, maturity, and independence—positive attributes! It is also a great avenue of attack when it comes to drawing him out and engaging him in conversation. If you know the inner workings of cars, or attributes of certain types of cars, this is a great launching pad to begin conversation on a topic he might be very comfortable discussing.

I extend this appreciation to other hobbies or part-time occupations that also require practical skills. He'll earn extra points if the work is outside of his father's business. I know it's a little unfair, but working for Daddy isn't something that garners much credit with me, unless I know his father and know firsthand that Dad really does make him work, and doesn't just tolerate him because he has to. Asking what he does, where he works, and for whom will reveal his standing at that establishment pretty quickly. Then you can decide how much merit you are going to award him for his efforts.

If he works for a friend of the family, that's still good news. Not many people will endure someone else's kid working for them and wasting their time and resources, certainly not to the degree that the father of the kid would. Although I'm not about to start planning a parade, I'm going to begin chalking up some pluses in his favor if this is the case. If I'd be quick to put black marks next to his name, I should be quick to acknowledge indications that he might be a good guy.

How angry is your daughter? How twisted is her sense of humor? If a guy shows up at your door smelling bad, it's possible that she'll do anything she can to make you mad or get your attention. There isn't a normal girl in the world who hungers for a filthy stench. Finding the best (most healthy and attractive) mate possible is so ingrained in her DNA that if she decides a smelly guy is a good catch, she either hates herself or hates you. I don't for a second think this will happen to a dad who has taken the time to read this book and align himself with his daughter early enough in the dating process to be a positive influence. So if it happens to you, the conclusion I draw is that she's got a serious (and respectable) twisted sense of humor, and you two must have an amazing relationship. If this is the case, go along with it. Make like you love the guy, send her on her way, and time how long the date lasts. I'm guessing she'll be back home within ten minutes.... Either that or she's headed to her best friend's house to make you believe she really stuck out the night with Stinky!

Number seven on the smell list is self-explanatory. If he smells of dead cats and dogs, immediately find a defense attorney who can defend you after you kill him. Please don't call me, though, I'll deny we ever spoke about this....

It surprises me, even now, when I think about how much information is available for you to decode in the first few seconds. There are a number of sources that say first impressions occur within five to ten seconds, but I think we get there quicker than that. I know that with practice, you'll be able to decide in one to three seconds whether he is a good bloke or not. A plus side to being able to do so this fast is that it allows you to begin formulating the questions you want to ask during the small talk from the door to the kitchen. You can't stop him from jibber-jabbering during that time if he chooses to do so; but let's be honest, you don't have to be a rocket scientist to answer his inquiries, assess him, and strategize as you walk. If you've got doubts about your skills, ask your wife how she does it. If you married above your pay grade, as I did, then she's clearly smarter than you and does it with you all the time. It's why we always feel stumped when tough questions get parlayed in our direction while we thought she was occupied chatting about tomorrow's to-do list. Not so, I'm afraid. She's planning tomorrow's agenda whilst simultaneously considering how to outflank you on a topic that was discussed last month, and compare your current answers with those of days gone by. I only need you to make small talk, walk, and plan for a few moments… so hold it together, man, you can do it.

In the following chapter, we are going to cover classifications and categories of signals. The magic ingredient when it comes to reading people is the ability to know which categories to place signals in. Some signals are conscious and voluntary, and others are subconscious and involuntary. For you to keep a handle on what's really being said, you'll need to be able to differentiate between them.

CHAPTER FIVE

Categories of Signals

"I just want people to accept me for who I pretend to be."

—Unknown

Your daughter's boyfriend will prove to be no exception to the above remark. But, as we are all comprised of many faces, we shouldn't be too quick to condemn him. Society practically demands that we manipulate our behavior to conform to accepted norms. From job interviews to family gatherings, most of us become extremely versatile at playing the version of ourselves that fits the events we go to.

As we get older, we all tend to show more of who we really are. It's exhausting to not be ourselves and we answer to fewer people. Junior isn't so lucky. Your daughter's boyfriend is going to show up to meet you, being the best version of himself that he can be—at least presumably. Once the first few seconds of analyses are behind you, you are going to need to begin holding a natural, easy-flowing conversation that doesn't have you staring at him like he's Sunday roast.

Each of us has our own unique habits. They help make up who we are, and anyone close to us knows which mannerisms tend to surface given a particular environment and its mood.

If I'm engaging in a joke and a good laugh with my family or closest mates, they have a good idea what that twinkle in my eye means—that somebody is getting their leg pulled. And if it's by me, it's getting pulled hard. I have nonverbal signals that accompany this lead-up, and also a certain way to give up the floor and let them start in on me. We all do. You may not have thought about what your "tells" are, but your best friends will definitely know what they are.

Before you can begin decoding Junior and figuring out his "tells," there are three guiding principles you need to understand to quantify his behavior: baseline, clusters, and context. I recently read a book that disagreed with attempting to measure a person's baseline of nonverbal behavior, how he or she communicates verbally nonverbally when not under stress. It was considered "too complicated" for the average person to keep track of, and too inaccurate to be deemed a science. I agree with the authors on one of these two points, that it isn't a science. The act of reading body language should never be termed a "science," as too much of it is ambiguous. Unless you are a psychic, there will never be a time when you can say with 100 percent certainty that you know exactly what is going on in another person's mind. However, if the circumstances are emotionally charged and the person experiencing the emotions feels the need to hide or mask them, there will be signs of the relevant emotion if you know what to look for. The body will leak signs of what the mind feels. Sometimes this will result in your knowing that what is being stated verbally and felt emotionally by the subject are one and the same, and sometimes it will mean the opposite is true. But without taking stock of what the person does when he isn't feeling emotional, we have nothing with which to compare it. They'll just be facial expressions, postural changes, and hand movements (or a sudden lack of) that don't mean a great deal of anything to us.

Just as you wouldn't scratch your ass or pick your nose in front of Her Majesty the Queen, and you probably would while driving your car or hanging with family, the boyfriend won't behave with you the way he does with his friends, or maybe even the way he acts around your little angel. And when I say "angel," you know I'm being facetious. As fathers, if we really believe our girls are angels, we are in for a rude awakening. Think back to the girls you liked to hang out with when you were young, and think about how they had fathers who thought their girls were angels. I ask you now, man-to-man, were those girls really angels? The boyfriend will be on his best behavior when he's with you—and this is something to keep in mind when you analyze his actions. He may be playing the role asked of him by your "little angel," in order to prevent you from knowing that she's a little hellion. But enough of this potentially devastating news in regard to your daughter, let's get back to baselines.

During your meeting, the boyfriend is likely concentrating on not screwing up, being super polite, and not giving away too much—with an end goal of your liking him. This will result in a polite face, generic subject matter, and limiting of his gestures, but they'll be done without his realization. They'll be a by-product of his determined state of mind. Unfortunately for you, these actions mask his baseline behavior. If he was with his friends, his nonverbal baseline would be vastly different than it is going to be with you. You are interested in the speed with which he answers the easy stuff. (Open-ended questions will keep him talking, and give you time to learn his speech pattern.) So: Is there a pause after you ask questions or does he go right into answering? Does he take a large breath before replying, even for the easy questions? What is his general breathing rate? What is the tempo and speed of his speech? How many times does he blink? The average rate for blinking is fifteen to twenty blinks per minute, but this can often increase during normal conversation to approximately twenty-five blinks per minute. Does he lick his lips, and if so, how often and at what speed? Does he clench his teeth and jaw? Most guys don't do this until they experience a strong emotional reaction to something, whether it's anger, stress, anxiety, or sadness (the jaw will sometimes clench in an attempt to fight back the emotion). Does he move his head in a relaxed manner? Head motion tends to become restricted when someone is feeling uncomfortable. Does he smile and does that smile engage the eyes? Genuine happiness will show at the corners of the eyes, not just the mouth. Depending on whether his answers are lengthy or cryptic, you might need twenty to thirty easy, socially expected (normal) questions prepared to keep things moving in order to gather all of this information.

It is my opinion that when most men try to be on their best behavior, they do less of the things they normally do. The face becomes less expressive, the arms and hands move less, and the feet tend to find one spot and stay there, locked down. In essence a person "shrinks"—and for once I'm not using this word in relation to the cold! Your job is to make him comfortable if this happens, and bring him back to life. If you don't and he remains frozen from the beginning on, your job comparing his baseline behavior with tough-question responses will be harder than it has to be.

But what if he's quite animated the first time you guys meet? Maybe instead of locking down and shrinking, his gestures are flamboyant and jovial. If so, throw him out immediately. No man wants his daughter dating a mime.... No, wait, that won't work either—your daughter would be extremely displeased. It could be that he's just a happy, carefree guy with nothing to hide.

Did you just roll your eyes?

It could happen, you know. He could be the rarest of commodities, a simple, nice guy. Or he could have read this book, studied hard, and decided that faking happiness is his best defense. Take nothing for granted. He could even intentionally be muddying the water by throwing every nonverbal signal in the book at you, all in an effort to make reading him more difficult.

With whatever he throws at you, or doesn't, be aware of clusters. No solitary signal will tell you everything you want to know. Instead look for groups of signals and pay particular attention to whether they gel together. A favorite signal of mine, one I specifically look out for, relates to the non-shaking hand during a handshake. Are the fingers relaxed, or has the greeter withdrawn the hand, putting it behind him so I can't see it? The person may be verbally telling me it's nice to meet me, but if the other hand is clenched, or, worse, hidden from sight, then the opposite might be true. Alternatively, if the greeter's non-shaking hand is forward of the body during the shake, with the fingers relaxed, and he is simultaneously leaning his upper body slightly forward, then the signals are a cluster of harmonious nonverbal indicators that his internal emotions match his words.

If you've ever had to deal with a slippery used-car salesman, then you've probably experienced signals that weren't working together well. Walking onto the lot of the dealership, you may have been immediately put off by his fake smile, and quickly thereafter put off by his predatory hand rubbing. When a fake smile (shown by a turning up of the mouth paired with eyes that aren't showing real pleasure) is combined with a slow rubbing or wringing of the hands, you know he's not happy to see you because you look like a great guy—he smells a deal. The fake smile is intended to put you at ease and make you feel comfortable talking with him about your "needs." The clusters of his signals will say, "I'm a shark moving in to take a big bite out of your wallet." If you can, compare the feeling you get from a used-car dealership with the one you get when going into a dealership where the salespeople aren't working on commission. You'd find it's a totally different experience. There is little chance that the salespeople at the latter will slither up to you, and the smiles there are more likely to be genuine. The clusters of signals these people display will reveal that they're genuinely interested in helping you find a good deal.

If you witness conflicting signals, then the mixed message is likely a bad thing. The general rule of thumb is to believe negative signals, not positive ones. The reason for this is that people often try to fake being happy when they aren't feeling it, but people rarely try to fake negative emotions when they are happy. Outside of playing poker or lying (which can induce stress, fear, or even delight—more on this in a moment), there are few times in life when someone has to hide his or her happiness. There are even fewer instances when a person needs to pretend to be sad, upset, anxious, or mad. The obvious exception to this rule relates to funeral workers. No one wants them showcasing that they're having the best day ever while Uncle Bob is being lowered into a hole.

In certain circumstances, lying can result in a feeling of superiority over the listener, and this emotion manifests as something Dr. Paul Ekman termed "Duper's Delight." When someone is lying and feels as if the listener is falling for his story, he might experience a sense of excitement. This can be revealed by inappropriate smirking—a one-sided curl up of the mouth—or smug contempt. Picture a killer talking to the press about his crime, feigning ignorance and proclaiming that he couldn't possibly have committed the crime because he isn't "that sort of a guy." He likely feels his story is convincing because the reporter hasn't stopped him or contradicted him... yet. There are so many cases of this, but I'm deliberately not mentioning any of the criminals' names as examples. I don't want to give them more attention or recognition than they have already received.

Let's say Junior is acting exactly the way you'd expect a boyfriend meeting Dad for the first time to act. He's showing nervousness (lip licking and elevated/decreased blinking) and excitement (shown by him clearly finding it challenging to not keep smiling—after all he is taking a fox out tonight), and your conversation is flowing. If you feel like you've got a good measure of the lad, then this is the perfect time to ask him a tough question.

"I talked with one of your friends last week and he told me something about you that's a little alarming. Have you done something in the past that I should know about?"

Suddenly he has tap dancers' feet, the smile retreats behind a grimace, and his hands disappear into his pockets. That's a cluster of nervous signals worth paying attention to. His fearful reaction might signify he feels caught. But keep in mind that this could be misleading! Even if the things he's considering aren't particularly bad, the apprehension produced by running through possibilities is enough to produce a cluster of nonverbal behavior similar to the ones that indicate guilt.

But what if you'd asked the same question and he hardly missed a beat, shook his head no, and kept the same genuine smile he had all evening? His hands didn't move, his feet stayed perfectly still, and other than a fleeting eyebrow flash of surprise that you talked with one of his friends, there's no change. Well, contextually, an eyebrow flash up would be perfectly normal. Fear shouldn't be. Of course, using the word "alarming" in your question was a harsher term than "interesting," "perplexing," or most of the other words you could have used. We'll get into what sorts of questions and terms to use in Chapter Eight, but my point now is that no matter how tough or innocent your question, if you change his baseline behavior and he displays a cluster of new signals, the dominant cluster will provide direction toward or away from further interest in that topic.

Context is defined by environmental, circumstantial, and conversational influences. Within the context of meeting you, Junior is being challenged environmentally (he's on your home turf) and circumstantially (he has to make polite conversation when he'd rather be out having fun with your daughter). He doesn't know until you ask your first tough question that he is going to be challenged by your inquiries, too! Maintaining a consideration for context is critical when attempting to interpret a person's behavior. If someone's behavior or reactions seem odd given the circumstances, chances are that this is because the person is reacting in a way contrary to what you would expect. Consider the mother (who shall remain nameless) with the abducted children who held a press conference begging for the safe return of her children. She claimed that they were taken from her during a carjacking, and had been missing for eight hours at the time of her public appeal. Contextually, we should see a woman at her wit's end, scared to death, in shock, terrified, and pleading for her children's safe return. Instead, she was partially smiling, and in awe of all the people searching for them. Her display was wrong in context of the situation. If you let the context of the questions (in addition to the circumstantial and environmental considerations) you ask Junior guide how you interpret his responses, you'll speed up interpreting whether what he displays is expected or unexpected. And if you see a cluster of signals that are unexpected, you will know that whatever subject triggered the response requires further questioning.

Now we need to be able to classify signals and understand why it is so important to do so. As we know, each of us is impacted by the circumstances (among other variables) that we find ourselves in. But our behavior is also impacted by the secrets we keep and the gaps that exist between who we are publicly and who we are privately. The more issues or baggage we carry around, the greater the likelihood that the signals we emit are confusing or at odds with what we say. In other words, the more screwed up a person is, the more screwed up he is likely to come across, even nonverbally. This should not shock you. Consider someone you have dealt with in the past who set your teeth on edge from your initial meeting. Something about how he behaved seemed contrived, forced, or just plain cuckoo. You may not be certain what it was he did to make you feel this way—nonetheless, he elicited a strong reaction from you that resulted in your disliking him immediately.

One of the most challenging aspects of interpreting other people's behavior is deciding whether what they displayed was planned (conscious) or unplanned (subconscious). Many gestures can be easily manipulated to support an intended message. But with so many to choose from, if the person speaking uses conscious thought to plan every signal, he will quickly become overwhelmed. The most accomplished communicators are relaxed and appear this way because their gestures flow smoothly, without the person actively considering/choosing them. As long as the speaker's internal emotions match what he is saying, the person's subconscious knows which signals are needed. If the person isn't relaxed and is trying hard to simultaneously control the flow of verbal *and* nonverbal information, it will show by ill-timed gestures that don't sync with the person's words. A person cannot consciously keep up with regulating words, volume, inflection, facial expressions, hand gestures, and body posture without looking crazy. It is simply too much! Even the best and brightest can control these only for a very short period of time. It will be easier for you not to think about whether his gestures are conscious or subconscious, but rather to appraise the timing of his signals and assess whether they match. More often than not, signals with too much premeditation appear contrived and are larger than necessary. Naturally occurring ones spawned by the subconscious stand out less and flow easily with the conversation.

Few people work that hard at controlling their gestures and nonverbal information. They believe that if they don't verbally share sensitive information, then no one will be privy to their innermost fears and problems. Others will tell you at the first opportunity how messed up they are, sharing details about themselves that we might not have wanted to know. Even though, as men, we often prefer not to be privy to others' baggage, when it comes to reading people, those who share too much have done some of the work for you. Still, if your subject is an extreme sharer, don't stop evaluating and assessing him. As frightening as this might sound, sometimes people share personal information quickly to prevent you from digging into them. What they tell you might be bad, but there could be more and it could be much worse. Use what they share, whether it seems like it's only a partial disclosure or the whole enchilada, as a starting point for your questions, and hope you don't have to dig too long or hard to find the root cause of their idiosyncratic behavior.

What about those who are in denial of their issues, or worse, haven't taken the time to realize that they have a cartload of problems? Their signals have a good chance of being mixed up, and their subconscious may act as a pressure valve indicator, releasing signals of inner conflict, guilt, anger, or frustration.

If Junior comes into your house carefully controlling his face and body, ask yourself why he's doing it. What is he afraid of revealing? If he plays everything up with large pantomime hands and facial expressions in some feeble attempt to muddy the waters and inundate you with hundreds of signals, you'll have to determine which antics to disregard so you aren't wasting precious brainpower trying to take in everything he is showing. Consider the root cause (or context) of what is being discussed to determine the most genuine emotion or display. Because, if you're like me, brainpower is a rare commodity and you won't have excess to waste. Assuming he isn't Robin Williams's cousin on crack, disregarding superfluous signals will keep you on track and not distracted by the pantomime of smoke signals he's employing.

Categories of signals:

1. Emblems
2. Illustrators
3. Adapters
4. Affect Displays and Regulators

Emblems

Emblems are some of the most widely recognized and widely used gestures, and can take the place of speech without the conversation losing meaning. As long as the recipient and communicator are of the same heritage and social background, there is little chance an emblem will be misconstrued.

The following list includes some of the more widely recognized emblems:

1. Headshake or nod
2. Shoulder or hand shrug
3. Hand(s) covering mouth (shock, surprise, or horror)
4. Thumbs-up
5. Two fingers raised for peace or victory (unless you're in England and facing the palm toward yourself, in which case it's going to have a totally different meaning than the one you intended)
6. Palm facing recipient (Stop... *in the name of love*. Come on, you know you started humming it....)
7. Side-to-side wag of the index finger (parents' go-to signal when they are out in public and can't yell what they really want to say to their kids)
8. Point of the index finger at someone (threatening, anger, accusation, or precursor to violent intentions)
9. Raise of the index finger high into the air (e.g., "USA is #1!"—which would be true if we stop modeling our economics and health-care policies on the failed European model)
10. Palms together (praying or hoping for the best)
11. Palms up (pleading, supplication, no idea, or confusion)

12. "The bird" (nationally acknowledged and understood as a mild indicator of displeasure)

If a communicator can relate something and no verbal explanation is required for the message to be understood, then it's likely that an emblem has been used. (If the people interacting are from different countries, then some of the meanings might change—and if you set off an international incident by using the wrong gesture, I will not be coming to bail you out.)

Kids are great to watch if you want to see emblems exemplified, in particular, shoulder, hand, and mouth shrugs (shown by the lips being pushed together and raised toward the nose while the outer corners of the mouth pull down). If my kids don't want to fess up to a crime (or admit they know one was committed), then I can expect to see an emblem in place of words. It is easier to shrug the shoulders or hands to indicate a lack of understanding or knowledge than it is to verbally say, "I know nothing," especially when it isn't true. If the crime is a low-stress offense, meaning that the punishment isn't going to be heavy, I can expect a smile to accompany the shrug within seconds. They won't start beaming at me or anything, it's more a cheeky smile, and no matter how hard they try to suppress it, the darn thing just won't stop creeping up their faces.

When it comes to partial or one-sided shrugs (hands, shoulders, or mouth), rather than typical, balanced displays, a one-sided motion can show a lack of confidence or belief in what the speaker has stated. For example, let's say you've just asked the young man if he is aware that your daughter is ranked the top female in the country for One Thousand Yards Target Shooting, and he replies he had no idea and shrugs both shoulders equally as he answers. The shrugging part of his response is congruent with his answer. He may even flash surprise (eyebrows up). But if he answers yes, he knew that, but only one shoulder (or hand) shrugs as he replies, there's a good chance he was clueless, but doesn't want to admit it to you. One-sided displays like this often correlate to a lack of conviction or belief in a statement. Hand shrugs are rotations of the hand at the thumb and can range from a small thumb twitch all the way up to an exaggerated, palm-up raising and turning of the hand.

Another indicator of the inner conflict that sometimes accompanies denials and lies is a headshake or nod in opposition to what is being said. When a person is verbalizing information that he knows isn't true, his subconscious isn't happy. The net result is that while his mouth is telling you one thing, his body is leaking the opposite. One of the ways it does this is head shaking (no) when what he is saying should be supported with a nod (yes) or vice versa. Occasionally, I'll be asked to evaluate a suspect's interview tape from an investigation (corporate and law enforcement). During the questioning, the suspect may deny knowing what the interviewer is asking about and all the while his head is nodding yes. Sometimes this is pronounced, and sometimes it is slight. As with all things related to body language, this wouldn't "prove" anything, but it would certainly warrant additional inquiry.

It is especially hard to attribute a headshake or nod (or verbal response for that matter) to a particular line of questioning if the interviewer asks a compound or multipart question. As soon as you complicate matters with complex questions, it becomes nearly impossible to identify which part of your question the person is responding to. Simple, one-answer questions are best when you are trying to pin someone down and find incongruencies between verbal and nonverbal responses. The more you feel a person (in your case, the boyfriend) is feeding you BS, the more important it becomes for you to simplify your questions. If what you observe matches what you have heard, then it should be okay to move on. But if things aren't gelling, it might be time for the car battery and set of metal clamps.

Illustrators

The next type of gesture on our list is the illustrator. These help define and bring scale, meaning, or emphasis to the spoken word. During your time bonding with your kids, you have witnessed how they behave when they are excited. Special attention should have been devoted to how they act when they are telling a story or explaining something. Did you ever notice how hard it is for them to keep their hands still? Heck, to just be still, period! My son is a nonstop mover, much worse than my daughters, generally speaking, but both my girls also have go-to gestures when they talk. Excitement brings flamboyant hand movements, facial expressions, and other body movements. If they are really happy, I might see all three, simultaneously, in the span of about three seconds. It never really stops, and looking on the bright side, it's a great way to cool off on a hot day, as that many hand movements create quite the breeze.

All of us, to some degree, use our hands during conversations and storytelling to help bring scale or life to a particular point or event. Hand movements are also among the gestures that disappear fastest when one is making something up and telling porky pies. Part of the reason for a decrease in hand movements when we are lying is that our brains don't think to tell our hands to move. They're preoccupied with managing the mental stress that comes from making things up, "recalling" things we have no real memory of doing or being party to. The fear of being caught in a lie also often induces a "freeze response," especially if the circumstances (e.g., a federal crime or a boyfriend knowing you might end him) are serious enough.

When we *actually* recall memories, emotions, sounds, and smells, a variety of things that were present the day they occurred are also recalled. All of those things are still real to the brain, so it doesn't have to work hard to slip back into the moment when they occurred.

Have you ever listened as a friend told the story of the giant fish he caught during that trip you couldn't go on? It's bad enough that you couldn't attend the bro-trip, but now he's constantly talking about the monster he reeled in. Each time he shares the story, his hands get farther apart. After he's told the story a handful of times, I'll bet that fish has grown to at least six feet in length, if it didn't start out there. Interestingly, during the first telling, if his verbal description of the length of the fish matched his hand illustrations, there's a good chance the fish really was that size. If the verbal and hand descriptions have never matched, even during the first telling, then he's probably been exaggerating the length all along, or quite possibly didn't catch a darn thing. It's up to you to decide whether or not to trash your mate's version of what happened during his fishing exploits. This is pretty harmless BS, so is it worth ripping him a new one just to show you've mastered how to tell truth from fiction? Unless your friend is an asshole, probably not. Just let him have it. Then maybe the next time you're making up a doozy about something, he'll be just as forgiving!

A lack of illustrators during question-and-answer time with my presumed guilty-of-something kids usually indicates that, at the very least, they know who did it, even if they weren't the perpetrators. As a sidenote, this situation tends to apply only to spontaneous denials. Rehearsed stories may well have more illustrators, rather than less, if the guilty party has had a chance to begin convincing himself or herself of the validity of the story. In the case of my kids, they haven't figured this out yet, but I'm sure it's only a matter of time. When I'm speaking to law enforcement groups, I encourage them to ask as many questions (again, individual not compound) as possible, and to try to encourage the person to expand on his answers. During this exchange, I want them to take stock of how many illustrators are used, especially when the interviewee is expanding on the particulars.

During training seminars, I often have officers get up and share three things about themselves. Two must be true, and one must be a total fabrication. The point of the exercise is to allow the rest of the room, all cops and investigators themselves, to ask questions and follow up on the responses while observing the nonverbal portions of the communication. No one likes to be put on the spot, and cops have an especially hard time being the focus of their peers, but this exercise allows them to learn an amazing amount of information in a very short period of time, both as interviewers and interviewees. The emotions they feel in the hot seat provide unique insight into the emotions most likely experienced by a suspect and how they can best exploit those feelings. Illustrators, even during a training class, become anorexic on the ground as the poor bugger up front feebly attempts to keep track of the details of the lie.

Similar to the lessening or lack of hand motions by someone telling a lie, there is a tendency for a person to control his hands or completely hide them during times of stress. Adults and kids alike often grasp their wrists behind their backs or shove them deep into their pockets. Occasionally, whether standing or seated, an individual will squeeze the fabric of his pants, giving the impression that he is holding on to a cliff edge. Sometimes it is quite comical to observe the degree to which people try to control all aspects of their movement!

Adapters

Adapters are like pressure release outlets for physiological responses the body experiences during times of stress, fear, or anxiety, or even just the dislike of something. To understand why the body leaks signals of distress, it is important to know what is happening internally when it does.

The body responds to stress and fear in a variety of ways. One is a surge of adrenaline in response to stimuli. This can be produced by something like a sudden loud noise, and in the case of one, the body reacts quickly. It might flinch, duck (shown by the head dropping between the shoulders), withdraw from the source, or do all three. And in these cases, the person might laugh at his own reaction in order to help alleviate the stress. In addition to adrenaline, nonessential blood vessels constrict and the heart rate and breathing increase so that primary muscles are hyperoxygenated and primed for response. This speeding up of the metabolism produces additional sweat secretion to help keep the machine at an optimal temperature.

In contrast to a sudden loud noise, there is the low-level stress associated with things like meeting Dad. The physiological responses to this might not be as severe, but could be similar. If he's not ducking or fleeing, Junior's body will find other ways to bleed off the tension. He might fidget, play with his fingers, tap his foot, lick his lips, blink a lot, stroke the back of his own hand, or merely freeze, stock-still. If you've done your job, building a moderate amount of rapport, the last thing he should be is in freeze mode. However, as soon as he realizes that he's not going to get by simply by using normal social pleasantries, he might panic and shut down. If you've strung together a series of probing interrogation questions—for instance, you mention your knowledge of his "sealed" juvenile criminal record—you might get such a response. A kid without a record wouldn't experience fear of any magnitude if you claimed to know this because he doesn't have a sealed criminal anything. He might laugh, look surprised, and wonder where the hell you got your false information from. He'll certainly verbalize that he doesn't have a juvenile record. And if this is the case, good for him—and for you, of course.

A guilty kid might initially react the same way, laughing and looking surprised, but his surprise would be blended with fear, and there wouldn't be a clear verbal denial of a record existing. In stark opposition to the innocent kid, he'll wonder where you got your "bad-for-him" information.

If you hit a home run with a question that strikes fear like this, and he's a bit of a cool cat under pressure, the only things that might freeze are his blink rate and eyeball movement. We all have a speed at which our eyes normally move, and we all blink at a fairly consistent rate, as referenced earlier in this chapter. Eyes that suddenly stop doing either at a normal pace are another adapter warning sign. They show that something has caught the other person off guard. Note, though, that the opposite could also happen. The blink rate could go through the roof. Stress and fear can cause a person's blink rate to double or even triple. Remember how President Clinton looked when he was on the stand during the Monica Lewinsky hearings? That was an impressive blink rate.

Swallowing could also be a chore. The body shuts down superfluous actions when it's prepping for something big, and saliva is something the body doesn't need during a sprint away from a threat. Thus, the tongue tends to become less pliable and cooperative when speaking or swallowing, and tends to stick to the roof of the mouth more than normal. The Chinese used to question suspects after making them take in a mouthful of dry rice. The theory was that the guilty would be more fearful than the innocent, and thus produce less saliva, causing the rice to stick in the unlucky bloke's mouth. I don't know about you, but if I'd been dragged down to the local Chinese police station for questioning and made to nibble on half a pound of dry rice, it would be dryer when it came out of my mouth than when it went in.

Adapters also manifest when the subject feels uncomfortable or dislikes something. It isn't only fear that drives the body to subconsciously vent internal feelings. A couple of years ago on a late-night talk show (I'll omit the names of the host and guest to protect Creepy and the poor female guest), I watched the female guest display a number of adapters as she struggled to get through the interview without throwing up. The host found the female guest extremely attractive, and as you guys know, we men don't think too clearly when we are blinded by beauty. In fact, we usually do what this guy did; we make one daft comment after another. And even though she wasn't laughing (genuinely) at his attempts at humor, he plowed on.

From the moment the guest walked onstage, she looked uncomfortable. Like many actors, she seems more comfortable playing other people than being herself. If you take her general discomfort and add to it a host who made her skin crawl, you've got the perfect ingredients to see some great adapters. She leaned well away from the host during the meet and greet on center stage, a gestural retreat indicating she felt crowded and uncomfortable. After the handshake and as they made their way back to their respective seats to begin the interview, she rubbed her palms on the back of her pants, literally wiping his touch off her hands. Once she sat, she immediately turtled up. This is a position we discussed earlier, in which the head is dipped low between the shoulders, lowering the profile and making oneself as small as possible. Other than when we are apprehensive, this is not a comfortable position; and given her world-famous status as an actress, her taking this position was particularly revealing. After a few minutes, she regained some emotional equilibrium and tried to make the most of it, but she was never happy or fully relaxed during the interview.

Something she didn't gravitate to was hair-stroking. This is another self-soothing gesture, and dates back to when we were children and our moms would stroke our hair to calm us down after a fright or fall. Men rarely have long enough hair to perform this gesture on themselves, without looking ridiculous, and instead pull at their ears, stroke their chins, rub the backs of their necks, or scratch their balls. Of course, scratching the balls has little to do with soothing and is done at every inappropriate opportunity just so we can check that they are still where we last left them. However, if the boyfriend suddenly starts making some *down there* adjustments, he might be giving them a last tender feel before he loses them to Dad's bolt cutters; in which case, he is definitely self-soothing and carrying a lot of angst.

Another adapter includes pulling at clothing to make slight and usually unnecessary adjustments. You might witness a man wearing a suit pull at his shirt collar during times of stress. A woman sometimes pulls at her skirt's hem if it is a short skirt, to cover more of her legs. Clothing adjustments aren't linked only with stress either. Self-adjusting or self-preening gestures like these can be used for a variety of reasons, including flirting or complete disinterest. Flirting is pretty self-explanatory, but gestures that convey disinterest need a little more explanation.

Sometimes preening gestures like picking at imaginary lint, flattening clothing, or adjusting how fabric lays can be extensions of the same attitude—superiority. The young man in your home may display this sort of behavior if you begin taking up too much of his time with your pesky questions. This won't be the sort of foreplay he's looking for. Lint picking and other gestures intent on displaying superiority or disinterest make my blood boil, and if one of my daughters' boyfriends ever displays them in my home, I'm going to bitch-slap him back to the Stone Age. I suggest you do the same.

My wife and I have a friend who proclaimed that the reason we were never granted a chance to meet her husband was because he suffered from debilitating shyness. As you might expect, we both thought this was crap. Eventually, we were proved correct. The meeting, when it finally occurred, was brought about by the friend and her insistence that her husband attend at least one of her get-togethers with us. My wife and I hadn't really felt we were missing out on much with his lack of interest in coming over, but we played along on the off chance that he really was just extremely shy.

Her husband hadn't even made it through our front door before we knew that his issue had nothing to do with being shy.

He was an arrogant asshole—plain and simple. The first sign of trouble was the head nod upward (minus an eyebrow flash) as he said hello. As you recall, showing the throat to strangers exposes one of the most vulnerable areas of the human body. It also displays a "you are beneath me" attitude by raising the nose so that the signaler is literally looking down his nose at the people he's conversing with. Once inside our home, his behavior didn't improve. He spread himself out on the couch like he'd been there a hundred times. Feigning interest in everything around the room and not once pretending to follow the conversation, he picked at his clothing, and stroked and preened his way through the next hour or so with barely a word spoken, even when the conversation was directed at him. It dawned on me after a short time that the problem wasn't us, at least not my wife and me. This was a power play to show his wife that her friends weren't important enough for him to need to be civil—or even fake it!

In my mind, this sort of nonverbal communication tells you up front what sort of person you are dealing with and things can only go downhill from this point on. Regardless of how well the meeting started, you will have already seen the best of what this person has to offer. Not surprisingly, our friend went through some trouble with her husband not long after we met him. Even though they had been married for only a couple of years, the pattern of behavior we saw in the short time he was in our home was enough for us both to know what might be on the horizon.

Although I don't know for certain what's come of their relationship, the sort of conduct he exhibited is often used by a soon-to-be abuser before he begins the abuse. It is part of a pattern of behavior that begins with isolating the victim from her friends. I share this with you now so that you can forewarn your daughter that a boyfriend who attempts to isolate her from her friends and family is directing her toward far worse trouble down the road. Although this is slightly off topic and is something I will cover in more detail in the final chapter, it's worth your time to learn the sequence of behavior a predator might exhibit, so you know why arrogant signals like these can be indicative of much more than mere cockiness.

The sequence of events for an abuser is:

1. Charm and Seduce – The abuser will be overly and unnaturally nice and attentive.
2. Isolation from Family and Friends – He will cause a slow and steady erosion of her desire to spend time with anyone other than him. Expect manipulative behavior, guilt trips, or temper tantrums when she wants to hang with others.
3. Threats of Violence – This tactic allows him to begin gauging her reaction to the potential of abuse. It's an "okay to proceed" sign for him if she stays with him.
4. Abuse Begins – She will think this is her fault. He has brainwashed her into thinking she can't do better and couldn't live without him, or worse, that he will kill her if she leaves.

It will be much easier to warn your daughter well in advance of what sort of body language an abuser might display than to try to convince her of the meaning of movements you've seen after the fact. By the time you meet him, his initial salvo of charm and seduction is well under way, and trying to convince her that prince charming is really a piece of crap will be virtually impossible. If she trusts you at this point, and you've already covered why these signals are alarming, she might be able to untangle herself without too much trouble. Any future evildoer she does meet will be ten times worse in a few months, when he has invested time and energy into his "project." If your daughter truly understands that your interest is her happiness and protection, she will hopefully listen and heed your advice. I recognize that if someone shows signs of feeling superior, it doesn't automatically mean he's a girlfriend abuser; but the male ego is a fragile creature and if the schmuck does this during your first encounter, why take the chance?

One other signal of perceived superiority that is definitely worth mentioning is the hands-behind-the-head position. I had an interesting meeting with a corporate CEO inquiring about my being a spokesperson of sorts for his new personal safety product. Our first meeting was enough to convince me that was never going to happen. I was welcomed into his office and given the $10 tour of all things important—family, accomplishments, acquisitions, and pets. Everything was displayed outwardly. The pictures, memorabilia, and awards were all facing out from his desk toward the door. This resulted in his facing the backs of more than two dozen frames while seated at his desk. If you happen to be lucky enough to work in your own office space and can decorate it however you choose, take stock of which way the pictures are facing. Pictures on my desk all face me. When I look up from my work, images of my wife and kids are readily available for me to appreciate. My pictures, awards, and certificates are not for anyone else. They are for me. When you display for others, you are showcasing ownership, control, and perceived status. This guy's office was a shrine to the things he "owned." During the quick tour he referred to his children as "the kids," not as "my kids."

"The kids are all stellar athletes and straight-A students. My wife, their stepmother, is proud, of course—when she's not out spending my money." Wow.... What a douche! He proclaimed ownership of his wife, and his money, but not his kids. The use of the word "the" in relation to his children is a distancing clue, and the tone of voice used for "my" wife and "my" money were the same: both implied ownership and control. Hell, there are so many issues here that it's hard to know where to start. But as we are going to cover more about the words people use later, I won't dwell. Once we sat and began talking details of his proposed plan, it was clear to me that I would never go for anything he offered, no matter how much money was on the table. The funniest part of this, if I had to find humor in it, was that he didn't really believe a word he was saying either. So at least I wasn't alone in thinking he was feeding me a crock of proverbial you-know-what. Each time I questioned him on specifics, he would begin tugging at his earlobe as he fumbled for numbers that would sound good to the layman—the layman in this case was me, of course. Earlobe pulling is another adapter and usually accompanies BS. As the words leave the person's mouth, his subconscious is already denying what he is saying. In an attempt to block the lies, his hands come up and partially shield his ears. If *a listener* does this, he might also subconsciously be trying to avoid hearing the lies. Either that or the speaker talks too much and he doesn't care whether what is said is true or not, he just wants the person to stop talking.

The final straw came during his delivery of the details of what I might earn from this little arrangement. As you might be envisioning, he leaned back in his office chair and placed both hands behind his head. He displayed complete and utter arrogance as he paused for dramatic effect, allowing me to, in his mind, sweat the vast sum of money he was about to offer for my services. I couldn't help but jump in at this point and excuse myself from the grand scheme. I quickly explained that this wasn't going to be something I was interested in being part of, before running, not walking, out of there. If I'd waited to hear what he was offering, I might have found myself saying yes to many Mr. Benjamins and selling my soul to the devil. In the end, it simply wasn't worth it. I trusted what I'd seen and deemed it not worth the aggravation.

Affect displays refer to the expressions of the face and movements of the body that showcase the intensity of an emotion. When we are happy, we tend to be more buoyant in our steps when walking. If Junior is skipping down your driveway, someone is a little bit excited about the night's upcoming festivities. If he comes down the driveway dragging his feet and looking as if he is heading to the gallows, there's a good chance he isn't looking forward to running the gauntlet that surrounds meeting you. Presumably this isn't a reflection on the date he is about to embark on with your daughter. He might have his arms rigidly down by his sides, or he might have one arm up, bent at the elbow, and across his waist, as if he is holding an imaginary shield in front of him, and still be bouncing lightly on the balls of his feet. This would be a good indication that part of him is worried about meeting you, or making a good impression during his date with your princess; but he is still positive everything is going to work out well. *Don't you love young optimism?* As we rarely experience a pure emotion, a combination of body language signals and facial expressions might be evident, and some of them may seemingly be at odds with one another. The only time I can practically guarantee he might be experiencing pure happiness, void of apprehension, is after he escapes your home safely. But initially he'll be a bit conflicted internally.

If you are able to get Junior to open up about something that was tough for him to deal with, but he doesn't express the normal corresponding emotions, either on his face or through his posture, then your BS detector should begin sounding like a Klaxon horn inside your head. If the story is sad, then his face should display that emotion; his shoulders might slump, and he'll likely look down at the ground while he talks. This is an example of affect displays being in sync with one's words. As the listener during this confession, you should encourage the exchange by mirroring his emotions back at him. If he looks sad, you should look sad; if his shoulders have slumped, so should yours. Just don't overdo it. Mirror his affect displays to around 25 percent. You'll want just enough visible empathy to keep him talking and not feeling like an idiot for sharing.

As painful as this might sound, I want you to pay attention to your wife and her friends the next time they have a get-together. If one of them is talking about something difficult, watch how the group takes on the expression of emotion appropriate to the conversation. Women are freaking brilliant at reflecting back, showing that they are not only listening, but also sharing the emotion of the speaker. They feel what the sender is sharing and naturally utilize affect displays as they empathize and sympathize.

Men, not so much.

If someone within an all-male group shares anything meaningful, he's likely to end up being ridden like Sea Biscuit in the final straight. Keep this in mind if Junior does share something. You want this opening-up if it's possible to achieve. Many of the things that make up who we are and how we behave derive from the hardships we have endured. Sharing is never easy, but it indicates a willingness to face issues, not simply ignore them. This is especially important if your daughter has started dating someone with baggage. She may have fallen hook, line, and sinker for his tales of woe, but if he's making them all up, then they aren't off to a good start, are they? If he isn't making them up and really does come with emotional challenges, then observing how he chooses to deal with them will help you decide how to interact with and support the two of them as they grow. It will also help with deciding how to handle him if things go tits-up down the road and you feel your baby girl might be in danger.

Working in collaboration with affect displays are regulators. This is another communication tool that men fall short on and women excel in. Regulators are the signals employed between communicators that control the ebb and flow of conversation. We might literally take a breath and partially open our mouths to indicate we have something to say. A hand or index finger might rise to show we are ready to interject. Similar to the aforementioned covering of the ears, if the speaker has talked for too long, the listener might orient his body away from the speaker to express boredom and a desire to change the topic. A much more subtle version of the body turn is a foot turning and pointing away from the chatterbox, even pointing toward the exit. With this, the listener is indicating his desire to leave the conversation.

The largest differences (in this context) between men and women unfold after the speaker relinquishes the floor to the listener. For men, this is usually the time to put forth ideas on fixing any problems brought up. This is done to facilitate a change of topic. It is all very black-and-white for us cavemen. Someone has a problem, a solution is presented, and the assumption becomes that the topic has then been dealt with, so it's time to move on! For women, the emotion at the heart of the issue is likely to become the focus; they don't just talk solutions. It isn't that a solution isn't discussed, they do that too—but they communicate and connect on so many more levels than men.

This is important for you to know when the boyfriend opens up to you about something meaningful. Unlike hanging with your motorcycle buddies, where emotions have no place at all, you must resist the urge to regulate or stop the boyfriend from speaking with your sage advice. Understanding affect display skills will not only make you a more effective interrogator, it will also assist you in all types of conversations with your nearest and dearest!

We have only scraped the surface of things when it comes to the expressions that you will want to master reading. The next chapter will begin opening your eyes to all the emotions the face can reveal.

CHAPTER SIX

Face Time

"A stranger loses half his charm the day he is no longer a stranger."

—Genevieve Antoine Dariaux

In this day and age, with social media being the way for us to share our lives and communicate, face time is a dying pastime. Generationally speaking, the current crop of kids, "Generation Z," is going to be the most disconnected in terms of reading each other, as their interest and obsession with texting, Facebook messaging, and other forms of electronic social interactions are on the increase. And yet nothing is more powerful than eyeball-to-eyeball connection time. There is simply no substitute for real life, real-time face-to-face interactions, and all the communicative nuances that accompany these events.

I truly felt my age when, during a presentation to high school kids, they informed me that e-mail was now deemed too slow! Their advice was to use only text or FB (Facebook) to share information, as those are as close to instant as is currently possible. *Currently possible?* Talk about a wake-up call. Not only was e-mail deemed antiquated and so "yesterday," but the kids were already anticipating a way to communicate that will be faster and more hip than text. Of course, in a way they were correct. Not long after that shock to my system, Twitter began coming into its own, and what's quicker to convey information than a mass tweet? I'm still slightly unnerved that even I tweet. Just saying the word makes me feel emasculated.

Faces are a powerful tool in the communication world. And yet so much of what they tell us is missed because while we are in the middle of communicating, it's difficult to watch what's going on and still hold an intelligent conversation. We tend to expend more effort thinking about how we are coming across or what our next comment should be, than on what is being said or displayed by the other person. On the rare occasions when we commit to really listening and watching, we tend to take on the appearance of a cop, staring hard at the perpetrator as he spins a tale of lies. The focus becomes so intense and void of life that the only thing moving is the person's tongue as it protrudes from the corner of the mouth. Watching and not staring is an art, and it's one you are going to want to master if you don't want Junior clamming up under the pressure of your gaze.

Dr. Paul Ekman is one of the highest-profile industry leaders on the topic of decoding facial expressions, and as parcel to this, gives insight into micro-expressions, ultra-fast flashes of real emotions that often leak before the communicator can mask them. Ekman began his research into facial profiling more than forty years ago in order to help doctors determine the risk of suicide in mental patients who might otherwise be released from their doctors' care. Ekman and his team expanded on Charles Darwin's claim that there are five universal facial expressions—anger, fear, disgust, happiness, and sadness—and added contempt and surprise to the list. Regardless of a person's race, age, gender, or location, he found that seven expressions universally display during corresponding emotional reactions. The emotions are:

1. Anger
2. Fear
3. Sadness
4. Contempt
5. Surprise
6. Happiness
7. Disgust

Because of my background, I have always been adept at spotting indicators of anger. I grew up needing to identify this emotion as early as possible because my health and well-being depended on my ability to do so—when my dad was angry, it rarely took long for him to get violent. My father had the world's shortest fuse and would often mask his anger before striking. Instead of the normal furrowed brow and glaring eyes typically associated with anger, he would neutralize his eyes and forehead, hiding the rage behind a blank mask. He also didn't show the snarl often used by those who attack, until the outbreak began. The only indicator his body sometimes used to reveal what was coming was compressed lips, firmly held together in a thin line of control. In essence, I had little to no warning of what was about to happen. Seeing the speed and surprise with which violence arrived trained me to expect outbursts from anyone at any time. Thus I became extremely observant, and defensive.

An extension of anger, at least from where I sat, was disgust. I often saw this displayed prior to the mask settling on my father's face, and occasionally I'd see it after a violent outburst. I don't know if this was a result of how he felt about letting himself lose control, or if it was his attitude toward me because I "forced him" to teach me a lesson. Either way, it's one of those facial expressions I recognize quickly even to this day, and it makes me mad as hell when I see someone display it. You probably know what disgust looks like. The nose crinkles up and the upper lip rises in an attempt to partially block the nasal passages in reaction to the "offending" smell, or person. Consider the person who merely made an appearance, and yet you find yourself withdrawing from him. Or the buddy who has the sort of party trick that makes your skin crawl, and performs it every time the guys are together.

As a child I didn't understand or recognize contempt. But when, as an adult, I began researching facial expressions and body language, it dawned on me that this was another expression I was quite familiar with. My father didn't use it as much as expressions of anger and disgust, but it was definitely shown from time to time, and, although as a child I didn't fully grasp its implications, I knew it wasn't a good thing. I know now that this emotion is often used when a person feels superior to his conversation partner. I've seen it used by accused murderers while proclaiming their innocence during TV interviews, by arguing husbands and wives, and at corporate networking events and parties. I even saw it flashed by a stand-in doctor during my annual checkup one year. I had asked her a question and she obviously felt it was a stupid one. Ironically, my regular doctor had specifically instructed me to ask this question if I didn't get to see him during my visit. Catching the contempt flash immediately set my fuse burning and I asked her why she felt the question was stupid, or beneath her. She was not happy. Of course, she denied any such emotion, while turning bright red and stuttering like a thirteen-year-old caught with his hand in the cookie jar. It was emotionally tough because she'd been called out on her feelings of superiority, and she knew she was guilty. If she hadn't felt contempt, she'd have had no problem denying my accusation.

It took a lot more effort for me to become proficient at recognizing sadness and fear than anger, disgust, and contempt. This could be attributed to the fact that sadness and fear weren't among the expressions I saw on a regular basis growing up. It could also be because, evolutionarily speaking, people are best at picking up signals that forewarn them of attacks. Fear and sadness herald little potential danger to the other person, and can often be missed because of this. Men, as you probably know, are far worse at recognizing fear and sadness than women. The next time your wife says something cruel enough to hurt, don't think she didn't see your crestfallen reaction, because she did. She's just mad enough not to care!

We are not all constantly flashing true emotions before attempting to conceal them. Most of us have nothing to hide. But under certain circumstances, hiding how we feel can be hugely advantageous. Unfortunately, we can only so quickly hide what we really feel.... There is often a microburst of emotion that displays before we are able to get it under control.

One of my questions during my meeting with the egomaniac (discussed in the previous chapter) elicited a microexpression of fear right before he threw his hands up, behind his head, again. Contextualize this response for a moment. I asked a question he didn't want to answer (fear elicitor) and that he didn't feel he should have to answer (feeling of superiority), and the hands went up, behind his head. Then he leaned back in his chair and displayed a macro-expression of anger by compressing his lips. He was likely unaware that his lips were giving away how he felt… and most people don't like having this pointed out to them. If he had been better at reading other people, he might have realized how pissed I was getting with his antics and changed tactics. But, as is often the case with people like him, he was too self-centered to take the time to learn how to read others, or consider how he might be affecting them.

A micro-expression of fear is most easily read from the lips. They draw back and slightly down at the corners. If the emotion is extreme, they may go way back until they practically touch the ears. The forehead may even crinkle. If these happen, you are seeing a full-on nonverbal admission of how much fear the person is experiencing. If you miss a display like this, you should only be communicating with farm animals, as human beings obviously aren't your thing.

Sadness is hard to fake. From time to time I'll have my corporate or law enforcement groups attempt to "fake" sadness, and this usually results in fits of laughter. What is commonly displayed is a pantomimed version of what the communicator thinks he should be doing. Lips droop, heads lower, and shoulders slump. Suddenly the conference room is full of adults resembling a class of first graders hearing they won't be getting recess. The facial nuance most often poorly enacted is the knitted brow, drawn up in the center of the forehead between the eyebrows. Faking it when the emotion isn't real is hard to do—hence the uncontrollable giggles.

If you find yourself hearing a sad story that pertains to an experience your daughter's boyfriend claims he had, but he physically displays little or no sadness, anger, or fear, you should be more than a little suspicious. If Junior is spouting a tale in your kitchen and, supported by the behaviors you observe, your BS detector is going off, don't stop him or call him out—play along. Ask him questions, and then ask more detailed questions. And keep nodding the whole time. Minor details in a story aren't usually particularly important when we are telling the truth because we don't feel the need to recount every nuance to support what we are saying. But if someone is lying, then providing imaginary details helps pad the story. They can also trip up the storyteller, as they are so hard to keep track of. If he's told the story before, he will likely end it the same way he's always ended it. Only this time he'll get the grilling that has been lacking. It's also possible that he hasn't verbally told the tale before and has merely rehearsed it in his mind. Finding no faults with what he thinks he is going to say, he likely doesn't expect others (you) to find faults either. But because details are often under-considered by a storyteller, if you ask enough questions about them, he will eventually trip up.

Most people think they are adept at hiding their emotions. Your daughter's boyfriend will be no exception. He is going to show up to meet you expecting the normal Mom-and-Dad interactions—then he gets "trapped" in the kitchen and grilled by a master reader of body language and emotions (that's you), and all kinds of things break loose.

I recently made an impromptu visit to the organizer of an upcoming charity event near where I live in order to ask a few questions about the fund-raiser. My participation in the event would be voluntary, and in his defense, he had no idea I had been contacted about being a part of things by one of the organizers under him. He also had no idea what I do for a living or that I'd recently been part of the cast on the shooting competition TV show I previously mentioned.

His approach to our introduction was less than enthusiastic, to say the least. Let's start with his flash of contempt.

Maybe I wasn't dressed in the manner he would have liked. As I feel no need to conform to anyone else's idea of appropriate attire, this doesn't bother me in the least. I know this rebellious streak is a leftover from my childhood, when I had to conform to my dad's will—or face the consequences. Like I said, a psychologist would have a field day with me.... I'm not saying I looked like a vagabond—I just wasn't in a golf shirt and slacks. He probably presumed because of my blue jeans and hiking boots that this Q&A session was going to be a huge waste of his valuable time, since he'd have to "chat with the likes of me."

When he presented his hand for the shaking, it was turned palm down, and came from a moderately high position. After the shake was complete, he didn't move back or off-center from me, he held steady while he asked what he could help me with, and looked miffed as he did this. He lowered his eyebrows, something people do to intensify glares, and his lips compressed slightly together, tightening his jaw. There was no hint of a smile. The expression wasn't necessarily meant to intimidate or outwardly display displeasure; it was probably just a representation of his inner emotions. I'm sure there are others who might have found the display unsettling, but after my childhood and Commando training, it takes a lot to unsettle me. I mostly observe displays like this with a detached fascination, and then begin using my own nonverbal signals to mess with the person as much as possible. That's how I get my jollies.

As you may recall, ventral orientation with another guy is hugely important if you don't want to seem too aggressive. Normal positioning after a man-to-man handshake would result in both parties moving slightly away from one another, and angling away. He didn't do this, so neither did I.

It doesn't take long for a face-to-face position to become extremely uncomfortable, and this was reflected in the amount his blink rate increased when he realized (subconsciously) that I wasn't moving anywhere. In territorial terms, people who habitually don't move or angle themselves away from others think this is fine because the other person will normally do it for them. They can easily be thrown into body language disarray when this doesn't happen.

Occasionally someone who is socially awkward might not move away or change alignment. These folks tend not to react when others don't back away either. They simply don't recognize that this sort of positioning is probably uncomfortable for the other person. The way to differentiate between awkward and arrogant begins with the knowledge that, statistically speaking, you are more likely to encounter someone arrogant. If you don't move away, an arrogant person, in contrast to an awkward one, will either back away himself or begin escalating aggressive displays. He might take up more space with his arms and hands, puff his chest out, elevate or lower his chin, or even thrust it forward, glare, compress his lips, bounce on the balls of the feet, or decrease his blink rate. If he performs all of these actions at the same time, you can assume it is on like Donkey Kong.

The lady who introduced me to the event organizer, Miss Sally, someone I had talked with before, began explaining why I was there. I hadn't said anything until this point. The only things I'd done were to slow down my blink rate and slightly lower my chin. This created a rather stoic, unmovable-object impression before my new friend, and inspired him to be the one to take a step backward and change our alignment. Like I said, it's how I get my jollies.

Now things got interesting. As Miss Sally told Grumpy about my recent stint on television, my time in the British Commandos, and my soon-to-be-released book, I went from a major inconvenience to his new best friend in seconds. What's really interesting is the attempt he made to maintain a cool, professional air while experiencing a newfound sense of excitement and more than a little surprise. He didn't display a micro-expression of happiness, he displayed a macro-expression of joy and visibly struggled to contain it. Out loud he said, "I think this is great, my event could really use your help." Notice "I" and "my" used together in a very short sentence, both bringing emphasis back to him. One personal pronoun would have been fine, even expected, but not two. Compare this with my first conversation with Miss Sally, who remarked, "The veterans are going to love having you take time to come and meet them." She was just as excited, but for different reasons. Her excitement was projected toward the guests of honor, not herself for organizing, or for bringing in a vagabond like me.

It is always a great idea when reading people to let what they say lend support to, or occasionally contradict, your conclusions. If you begin second-guessing your deductions, the person's words might confirm what your gut is telling you. You will be amazed at how often you are correct.

The last expression my new friend displayed occurred during Miss Sally's explanation of my day job, teaching body language interpretation to corporate and law enforcement groups around the country. Would you like to guess what he then flashed? If you said fear, you are correct. It was an extremely quick emotional reveal, but it was there nonetheless. One thing I've learned over the years is that most people really are on the up-and-up, with normal but private idiosyncrasies they wouldn't want to share with the world. I'm no exception. And the thought that someone might be able to figure out what those things are is very unsettling. But most people, fortunately enough, don't need to worry about me seeing their issues. It is exhausting to really "read" someone, paying attention to every detail of what he does or says, so for the most part I don't drill down on folks unless I'm given a reason to do so.

What I'd love for you to derive from this is how much information was available from his facial expressions. There were body language indicators to support the flashes of emotions, but they were supporting players. If all I'd been watching was his body language, I'd have missed vitally important information about his state of mind.

The face is made up of forty-three muscles and can literally be contorted and shaped in thousands of ways. Aside from the seven universal facial expressions that are flashed either as a meld or singularly, there are also a multitude of messages the face shares as voluntary gestures. These gestures are learned or self-developed. I sometimes raise one eyebrow when I'm skeptical about something. I also do it when I'm messing with my kids. I picked this up from my mother, who did the same thing.

Now, to take it back to Junior, let's say that during your first few minutes interacting with Junior, he tells you about his family, pets, and how he met your daughter. During this time he maintains 40 to 60 percent eye contact with you. That would be a reasonable amount of looking you in the eye while talking. (During listening, he should be attentive to the tune of about 80 to 90 percent of the time.) While encouraging him to let loose every morsel of detail, observe how long is "normal" for him to hold eye contact with you before breaking, his standard blinking rate, and whether his posture is relaxed or stiff while he talks. This is a good time to ask questions about his grades, college plans, clubs he might be a member of, idea of the perfect job, girls he's dated before, and run-in with the law, etc. Presumably he answers everything up to the questions about his past girlfriends or his run-in with the law admirably. He hasn't hit you with too much or too little eye contact, and his pauses and verbal fillers are minimal. But then, as he attempts to find the right answers to your final questions, he begins sounding like he has terrible ADHD. And as he explains the girls and/or his misdemeanor offense, he doesn't release your eyeballs from his gaze. Alternatively, maybe he suddenly becomes extremely interested in the laces holding his shoes together and won't look at you at all. If one of these happens, you'll have witnessed a change in his baseline eye contact, with it going below 40 percent or above 60 percent, and this is important to note.

Most of us might assume sustained eye contact from a speaker is a positive thing, and often it is, but not always. Too much eye contact can indicate someone is lying. In this situation, the liar watches the listener intently because he's looking for a hint that the listener doesn't believe what he's saying. Similarly, if a person very suddenly starts staring a listener down, it might be because he's willing the listener to believe what he's saying. When someone is being honest, he doesn't have to work that hard at being convincing because what he's saying makes complete sense to him. It feels natural because it is natural. But when someone makes something up, it sounds phony even to his own ears, and he compensates for this by trying to force the information to be believable. Extended contact is one way to achieve that. In part this is because for many, many years, it has been drummed into our heads that good eye contact is indicative of honesty and trustworthiness. This is one of those old wives' tales, and a load of gobbledygook. It misdirects us from what we should be paying attention to and can prevent us from comparing what we are seeing with what we were seeing five minutes before. In addition, or instead, it could mean he's been scared into a freeze response as he relates the story to you. He's concerned you'll think he's a raging nut job and ban him from dating your daughter. Depending on what he has confessed to doing and how he confessed it, you might want to do just that. Or, you could reward his honesty, letting bygones be bygones, and allow him to date your daughter. It will come down to how honestly he communicates and how you feel about what he's said.

Unless he is an accomplished liar and feels next to no guilt or remorse, there's a good chance that if he stares you down, he might also be swallowing a little more frequently than before, when you took note of his baseline swallowing frequency. As the stress of being less than honest causes adrenal secretions to begin leaking into his system, his mouth may dry up. Licking his lips, an attempt to stimulate saliva production again, would hint at this. If he has been in panic mode since he arrived and you're not even sure what his baseline behavior is, then I want you to raise your eyebrows slightly, and with a small, warm smile gracing your face, nod appreciatively as he speaks. Raising the brows slightly conveys the "I'm not a threat" message. Smiling as you nod encourages him to keep talking. And hopefully, this combination will help him calm the fudge down.

Avoiding eye contact or having shifty eyes is one of the most common traits people assume reveals someone is lying—but they're wrong in this assumption. People can suddenly go shifty for a whole bunch of reasons, including feeling majorly humiliated about having to discuss something one would rather forget with the father of his girlfriend. Of course, if Junior begins performing a tango with his eyes, stuttering on his words, retreating, fidgeting with his hands, and exhibiting all kinds of panic signs, then you're witnessing a cluster of things, and clusters are always great indicators of emotions. If his behavior, eyeball movements included, deviates from his baseline and is accompanied by other signs of discomfort, then you're observing multiple signs of stress, and it's worth investigating further. But this still wouldn't mean he's definitely lying. Identifying lying with any certainty is incredibly difficult, and most people, even those who tell you they're great at it, more often than not really suck. I am more of a fan of combining what I see nonverbally with pinpoint listening to the words a person uses. I don't rely on any single (observing or listening) skill to determine the veracity of information. Instead, I look for deviations from one's normal behavior to decide whether he is experiencing expected or unexpected behavioral reactions to a topic of conversation. If you see a cluster of unexpected signals *and* hear odd terms and phrases, you stand a much better chance of recognizing lying. Never rely on one assessment skill. Use them all and you'll be a much better interpreter of whether you are hearing the truth—or not.

What if he is angered by your questions? Well, we all react differently to stress, adrenaline, fear, and dads who ask difficult questions. His reaction could be indicative of a guilty conscience rearing its ugly head, or of him feeling attacked because of his past crimes. One thing it is not normally representative of is innocence. You haven't accused him of anything yet, you are merely asking questions about his past. The innocent don't have anything to hide, and as such don't usually become angry.

Perhaps the boyfriend is temperamental and anger was his response to other situations where he felt attacked. In the past, this response may have worked as a mechanism to scare away inquiries from less-committed individuals. It won't work with you. If you find a nerve, dig, dig, and dig some more.

Your daughter might be able to shed light on this behavior if she has been on the receiving end of his anger. If her own queries into his past elicited the same response, then you've both witnessed his potential for angry outbursts, and you will need to explain to her why this could become a major issue with him down the road.

Be aware, though, that accomplished liars might not display any of the discussed indicators of deception. This is another one of the reasons it's so hard to spot a liar. The stress the rest of us feel while lying is absent in the more practiced bullshitters, and this can result in a distinct lack of physiological signs. Many nervous body language and facial indicators might be absent because the physiology that creates them is missing. This sort of person is commonly referred to as a sociopath, and we are going to cover more about this in Chapter Seven.

In Chapter Five, we discussed emblems, such as the head nod and shake. We touched on how the subconscious mind can cause a person to nod his head "yes," when he really should be showing "no," or vice versa. Another way to spot bull is eye-blocking. Extended blinks during a conversation could mean you are boring the crap out of the other person and he is growing tired. Or if he is the one talking, that a part of the information he just shared wasn't accurate. When this happens, the eyes close for slightly too long because the person is blocking out the moment; not seeing the listener or the environment during the lie can make it seem like it didn't happen.

In the same way a gestural retreat (leaning or moving the trunk away from the listener) provides a feeling of escape, so can a momentary eye block. This movement is usually involuntary, a subconscious retreat.

I also sometimes see an extended eye close when someone is attempting to be overly emphatic, as if what he just said should be the last word on a topic. One of the best places to see this emphatic signal is in commercials. The "everyday people" who are hired to convey appreciation for a product often use it as part of their "please believe me" repertoire. Once more, I'd love for you to watch a stretch of ads without their sound. Wait until you see someone talking to the camera perform an eye block or blink for too long, and then watch the ad again, but with the sound on. I'll bet you a bag of marbles that the person is attempting to sell you something by appearing as forthright as possible. This isn't to say the person doesn't believe in the product, but it's so much like pantomime that I wouldn't buy anything from the person.

An extension of the eye block (blink) is a hand that keeps finding its way back to a position that blocks or obscures the talker's view of the listener. There's a moderate chance that this won't even be a fleeting block. The hand may come up to "scratch" the eyebrows, and then stay there, massaging the skin and hair. Not only could this be an indicator that the speaker doesn't want to see the listener, but if the hand remains and continues gently rubbing, he may well be self-soothing. This sort of pacification can indicate anxiety, stress, fear, or shame. You need to determine why he suddenly feels the need to "soothe" himself.

Years ago, one of my self-defense clients asked me to teach her how to kill someone—*if she absolutely had to*—with bare hands, knives, or improvised weapons. Until this point, her interest in self-defense seemed on par with most women's interest in the subject. It seemed like she took the classes for physical exercise, nothing more. But with her question, she slowly explained how she had always wanted to know how to kill if she needed to. She started by inquiring about my knowledge of improvised weapons, knives, and guns, and then moved on to ask about the potential danger of one's bare hands. She especially wanted to know if there were skills a woman could learn so she could kill without weapons. When someone is making a confession or asking a tough question, the person often asks, as she did, with a casual lead-up and the most difficult, important, and emotionally charged part last—as if the person wants to distance himself or herself from it. For my client, that part was how to kill with her hands.

My male clients often asked for this information and rarely had anxiety doing so. My female clients were another story. I had a couple of women ask how to kill, and I pretty much always shared what I knew. The chance that a woman spontaneously loses self-control in a moment of extreme anger or unhappiness is slim. This is a reason why I respect when women carry guns (when/where they are legally allowed to do so). It levels the playing field.

When my client asked how to kill, she did several things:

1. Lowered her head slightly and looked down for a moment with her eyes (indicative of embarrassment or guilt)
2. Blocked her eyes by touching her eyebrow
3. Smiled an upside-down smile (a blend of attempted levity mixed with a little fear and sadness)
4. Protected her throat (a sign of feeling vulnerable)

Remember that the stronger the emotions or internal conflict had when an uncomfortable subject is broached, the greater the likelihood that multiple signals revealing the discomfort will be used. I will never judge a woman for asking this question, but I don't think she knew that when she asked it.

If the woman had exhibited these signals while making a statement, not a question—e.g., telling me she already knew how to kill with her hands—I would have interpreted them differently. But in context, they presented a vulnerable, ashamed, and slightly afraid manner. I hadn't seen her smile often, but when I had, it had never been the kind where the corners of the mouth draw down, in opposition to the rest of the mouth. If a person smiles this way, you should proceed gently. I said, "May I ask why the interest and need to learn those skills?" As I asked the question, I tilted my head slightly to the side, mirroring her position. She momentarily smiled the upside-down smile, but within seconds was fighting back tears. This was not a woman prone to dramatic outbursts. She was struggling with something very personal, and my deductions from the signals she had shown were being validated. She paused for about five beats longer than a person would usually take when giving an answer, indicative of an internal struggle and consideration of much she should share. Instead of trying to verbally prompt her into answering, I lifted my eyebrows slightly, maintained my head position, and began slowly and minutely nodding a nonverbal affirmation that I was listening, empathetic, and ready for her to share as much as she was comfortable sharing.

She drew a deep breath, and then the floodgates opened. She had moved several times in the past three years because of a stalker she had picked up at her old job, and she was worried he may have found her again. She hadn't seen him yet, but little things had been occurring that had made her uncomfortable, and she felt like she was constantly being watched. At the precise moment she said "being watched," her face flashed fear and anger. She suppressed the emotions reasonably quickly, but I felt it was done more out of a desire to control her feelings than to hide them from me, as they were macro-expressions, not micro-expressions. The congruency between her verbal and nonverbal messages couldn't have matched more perfectly. I'm going to cover more about this woman's story in Chapter Ten, so that you and your daughter understand why her gut instinct was so important, and why, as I've told you before, you should always be in tune with yours.

My client's facial expressions were indicative of something not being right, inner turmoil, anxiety, and vulnerability. Once I heard her story, I was hell-bent on teaching her everything I could about fighting off an attacker, weapons, guns, escape, and evasion, and where to stick an electric cattle prod to achieve maximum damage if need be. If I hadn't been quick enough to spot the signals of distress, I might have blundered through my response and not given such thorough training.

Sincere emotions are often displayed fractions of a second before the words materialize. If my client had displayed fear and anger post having shared that she felt like she was being watched, I may have doubted her sincerity. I wouldn't go so far as to say she was making the story up, but I'd have been a long way from truly convinced. If she had displayed the facial expression marginally earlier, I would have believed her feelings were as real as I did when she displayed them at the same time she spoke of the stalker. The brain works about four times faster than the voice box, and early displays support the words about to be shared. Late emotional displays are cause for scrutiny. To me this shows that it is only after the speaker hears his or her words that the person begins to consider the emotional tone or context that should accompany the message. If a person is really feeling what he or she is saying, then the face, body, and energy reflect the spoken words as they come out. If they don't and the signals arrive late, then there's a disconnect between the verbal and emotional messages, and the speaker might not be feeling the professed emotions. It is easy for a speaker to merely pay lip service to emotional declarations, especially if the person is making the whole thing up, so you must be especially cognizant of this potential if you want to become proficient at decoding the boyfriend.

Not too long ago, there was an interview with Syrian President Bashar al-Assad. The interview followed the poison gas attack in his country against his own people. Women, children, and men were attacked using sarin gas, and thousands died as a result. The interview was supposed to be an opportunity for the Syrian president to come clean about having chemical weapons, something he had denied for years, and to confirm his agreement to uphold the requests of the international community and destroy the weapons of mass destruction. Fox News reporter Greg Palkot and Fox News contributor and former US Representative Dennis Kucinich posed the questions. Bashar's nonverbal behavior and lack of congruent responses made my skin crawl.

A small, nonverbal error made by Greg Palkot was to keep his reading glasses on, but pushed halfway down his nose while he was asking questions. Don't ever leave your glasses on while interviewing a subject if they sit so low on your nose that you are forced to dip your face forward to peer at your subject over the rims. Lowering one's face like this makes the glasses wearer look angry, as it lowers the brows and promotes a "glare," and this can hinder an open, honest conversation. This is something to keep in mind before you meet the boyfriend.

One thing Palkot's glasses may have been partly responsible for was Bashar's use of his index finger. Bashar used it only once during the questions from Kucinich, but during Palkot's questions, he used it constantly. The index finger can be used like a baton, swinging up and down to bang one's point home or indicate extreme displeasure or anger. It can also be used to show frustration, and angrily point at a listener, in which case it may be a warning to back off. The person may feel attacked and be about to attack, himself. If the boyfriend uses his finger constantly, this gesture is a giveaway to what he's likely feeling.

Now to get back to reading faces, some months ago, I was fortunate to be part of a training program for a law enforcement and fraud investigations division in Seattle. My presentation and those of a handful of other speakers would conclude the investigators' three full days of training. I never trust that my flights to events won't be delayed or even canceled, so when possible I arrive the day before my session. This was another one of those occasions when I'm especially glad that I did. I arrived a day early and discovered that the person who'd be speaking before me was Glenna Trout, a consultant and expert on personality profiling based on facial reading. Until this time I had very little exposure to the topic of facial profiling, so I was excited to find out that I'd be able to watch her present.

My intention was to stand in the back of the room during Glenna's presentation and quietly observe. Upon arrival at the event the afternoon before, I found Glenna doing the same thing I intended to do during someone else's presentation. During the break, we struck up a conversation and she asked if I'd mind her taking my picture and using it as part of her presentation. I suddenly felt just like those poor folks I call up in front of their peers during my presentations—slightly vulnerable, transparent, and definitely on the spot. What could I say? No? I asked her to please be gentle with her appraisal of me and acquiesced to her request.

As part of my application to compete on *Top Shot*, there was a four-hour psych evaluation test, followed by an interview with a mental health doctor. I had to pass the test before being accepted into the competition. The test was exactly as you might expect a psych test to be: many, many recurring questions designed to elicit true-to-who-you-really-are responses. You can't fake it, as the damn thing is so long, with so many similar questions. It wears you down to the point that you just answer honestly and let the cards fall where they may. This is especially stressful if you already know you are a little wacky and are concerned that any shortcomings might exclude you from competing.

During my follow-up interview with the clinical psychologist, I discovered a few things about myself:

1. I control a lot of anger, which led the doctor to deduce that I'm very disciplined.
2. I'm very suspicious, a defensive mechanism developed from childhood.
3. I'm feisty as hell, much like other former servicemen. In her words, "You are the last person of this current group of competitors that I would want to poke or antagonize in any way.... I think someone who did that would only get one or two chances before all hell would break loose."

4. I use humor as a shield to keep people from getting too close to me, but those who are allowed close are in for life.

It's weird to have someone evaluate you so succinctly, and be able to get straight past the outer shield. I asked her as I entered her office, before receiving her diagnosis, if I was going to need a box of tissues before we started to talk. She politely laughed, and then, without making any sudden arm movements, shared her findings.

Fast-forward two years and my face is up on a large overhead projector for the entire law enforcement group to analyze. I'm surprised no one got up and left. Glenna began by splitting my face in half, and then began explaining that in Chinese face reading, the left side of the face is the Yang and the right side is the Yin. This equates to the left side of the face being the private part of who you are; the right side is the side you show to the public. It all seemed very voodoo to me, but then I was still worried about what might be coming next, so I kept my sarcastic comments to myself. Then she started getting down to the nitty-gritty. Using a mirror image of the left side of my face, she completed my face by reproducing the left side again, but this time in place of where the right side should have been. Now my whole face was really my left side replicated to give the impression of what my face would look like if it was all left. Guess what? She began her analyses in front of the group, asking for me to agree or disagree with what she deduced from the lines and configuration of muscle and bones that made up the left side of my now entire face. These were her findings:

1. Terry is probably very disciplined and driven.
2. He has a tendency to carry anger issues.

3. He would rather die than fail at anything.
4. He has a very pronounced sense of right and wrong.
5. He isn't someone I would like to cross, but if he calls you a friend, then it's most likely for life.

Imagine my surprise! A four-hour psych evaluation and interview with a doctor of crazy found roughly the same information out about me that Glenna deduced from a photograph. An additional golden nugget of information she validated for me (the amount of information she had was staggering—she's been studying this discipline for more than thirty years) was my habit of looking into a person's left eye during a handshake. I hadn't realized that I did this instinctively, until she pointed it out during her talk. She had observed me looking into her left eye when we'd introduced ourselves.

As you begin reading faces and understanding the correlating emotions, keep in mind that what you see in a person's left eye better reveals who he is than the more commonly observed right eye does. (Most people are right-handed and right-eye dominant, causing them to look at the other person's right eye when shaking hands.) If you see a friendly face during your handshake, make sure to observe the left eye and whether it reflects the emotion as strongly as the right one. If the person is naturally guarded or aggressive, happy or sad, the left eye is more likely to reveal this. I am left-handed and left-eye dominant, so my fixation with appraising new encounters through what a person's left eye tells me suddenly made sense. I have always been somewhat suspicious of people and have rarely accepted that what is being shown on the face is a true representation of real emotions. But I didn't realize my conclusions were derived from a quick study of the left eye. I was amazed to find this out.

If an opportunity presents itself and you are able to secure a picture of lover boy before you meet, but you don't have time to Photoshop a mirror image of the left side of his face over the right side, then take one of your wife's small makeup mirrors and place it along the center line of his face. Angle the mirror back and forth until you've managed to even out the left-side reflection into as normal a replication of his entire face as possible. It might be a perfect extension of the public (right) side, or it might showcase issues upon issues. This project will give you warning of what to expect when you meet him.

It never hurts to study up on why facial profiling is such an accurate tool for reading someone, but in case I can't convince you to acquire one of my favorite books on the topic, *Face Reading in Chinese Medicine* by Lillian Bridges, then at least follow Glenna's blog at http://itsallaboutface.wordpress.com or look into attending one of her seminars. You will not regret taking the time to add this skill set to your boyfriend-reading arsenal.

As I mentioned before, other resources for you to use to improve your facial-reading skills, especially for reading micro-expressions, are http://www.paulekman.com and http://www.humintell.com. I have completed nearly all of their courses and still revisit the sites to brush up from time to time, as I believe it is a perishable skill. If your daughter knows you've spent your valuable time mastering topics like these, it will make your findings much more valid if you have to share some scary information about her new flame. Remember that if after all this study and practice, you don't see anything to be concerned about but you still don't like him, then at least you've put in the work (on her behalf), and voicing concerns based on your efforts will carry more weight than just the words of a typical anal-retentive dad with a grudge. Another place to observe facial expressions, as well as body language, is YouTube. It has millions of interviews with a multitude of different personality types. With it, you can pause, rewind, and take your time watching every nuance of communication, and break down each part of the message being shared—both the intended and the accidental.

Listen carefully to the interviewers' questions and watch the interviewees' facial responses during the delivery of the questions. I am often frustrated by how television cameras pan back to the interrogator, just as he or she asks the most interesting questions. This will probably drive you nuts, too. The initial emotional response to a question is often the most honest part. It is also often the most fleeting. When, from time to time, the camera doesn't move off the subject, every aspect of the person's response is captured. All you have to hope for then is that the interviewer is a professional and asks only singular, rather than compound, questions. Then that flash of anger, sadness, fear, disgust, surprise, contempt, or even happiness is definitely a result of the question, and the subconscious mind is revealing its true sentiments.

In Chapter Seven, we are going to look at personality concerns and traits. We'll look at personality issues and warning signs that Junior might be a train wreck in the making. Then you can implement a plan outlining what your daughter needs to look for, to avoid him like the plague he is.

CHAPTER SEVEN

Personality Concerns

> "The wise man does at once what the fool does finally."
>
> —Niccolò Machiavelli

Political correctness is sure to be the death of modern society. If it hasn't unraveled commonsense thinking enough already, it's certainly dragged us a good way down the path of no return. Most people fear calling a spade a spade enough to shy away from outward declarations, at least ones made beyond the security of our own homes. In private, however, politically incorrect pictures, quotes, observations, criticisms, jokes, and YouTube videos grace inboxes or Facebook accounts on a weekly basis. More often than not I laugh aloud at the ones I get, before swiftly quarantining them into my electronic trash basket. God forbid I share them beyond the security of my four walls. Even speaking about God can yield a thousand complaints. "Free speech" is a misnomer for what we have. We are really able to practice free speech only if one touts the currently accepted PC diatribe. Beyond that, the potential repercussions of saying something that might upset an obnoxious few paralyzes the majority. Maybe it doesn't matter, though, because the majority is too busy working their asses off to enjoy their

First Amendment freedom. Ironic, right? But I draw the line at not being able to call an asshole an asshole.

These days rude, abhorrent behavior is sugarcoated in a manifesto of glorified titles and excuses. I believe that if someone wants to act like an idiot, we should be afforded the freedom to call him out on that behavior. If the person feels he has the right to say something direct and demeaning, he shouldn't be surprised when the retort is scathing and belittling.

My wife and I recently agreed to let each of the kids invite a new friend over to play. As we had only recently moved into our new home, this was a big deal for the kids and a big deal for us—it also meant my honey-do-list was extremely close to completion. Pictures were hung, mirrors aligned, furniture organized just the way it should be. The nest was ready. Each of our children provided the phone number for a friend to have over and my wife began making the calls. With my British accent, it's easier to let her perform the on-air communications. Well, that and the fact that it's more socially acceptable for moms to call and make the invitations than dads.

We called one of our son's friends first. His mom was *very* excited about the invite, and in retrospect that should have been a warning. Parents are usually happy for their children to attend playdates; but let's face it, they require scheduling, driving, and planning around what was already going to be a busy weekend of chores, cleaning, grocery shopping, and catching up on recorded episodes of *Sons of Anarchy*. That last one can't only be me, right? Playdates aren't something that typically elicit a great deal of excitement from the moms and dads—the kids, yes, but rarely the parents. However, she was over the moon.... Then she let the reason for her excitement slip: "If you don't mind, I'd love to bring my youngest son, too, and visit with you myself. They don't get invited to play very often, so this would be great. Plus, we could just hang out and get to know each other while all the boys play. Wouldn't that be fun?" Err, no. But, okay. I happened to be within proximity of my wife during the call, and she began mouthing "WTF" with a helpless look on her face. But being a nice person—albeit wishing it had been me who made the call—she agreed and hung up. Then all our plans for the play day went up in smoke. My wife was going to be entertaining more people than planned—and the guests included an adult woman.

It didn't take long after the mother and her sons arrived for the reason they needed friends to become obvious. She was bat-shit crazy, and so was her youngest son. Her excuse for his screaming, temper tantrums, sulking, glaring, freezing in place, drooling, and other spontaneous outbursts of ridiculous behavior was courtesy of the best medical explanations Google has to offer. She'd self-diagnosed him with having a little bit of everything, ADHD/ADD/AC/DC. I think this helped her cover all of the bases. At one point he came upstairs from playing in the basement and screamed at his mom that he wasn't happy because his brother and our son, Aidan, wouldn't make the Wii console let him win anything. Aidan let me know later that when the little tyke had yelled at him and his brother that they weren't playing fair, he was playing alone. Immediate clues I'd seen when the family walked in that indicated that the mother and son were bonkers are ones you'd be able to recognize from my lessons in the last chapter. For one, the mother's blink rate on arrival was too fast. Her boys had the opposite problem. The younger one showed a little too much white of the eyes (think of Charles Manson's frantic eyeballs), and had a blink rate far too slow to be normal.

So what happens when Junior is standing in your kitchen and has some sort of crazy eye situation going on, and you are at a loss for words to explain why your daughter brought this oddity home? Well, the first possible justification is obvious, she just likes weird—or at least she likes his brand of weird. Other possibilities are that she is shy and doesn't like to talk about herself and he's the type who likes to talk only about himself. Or maybe she doesn't think he's strange.... If she has been sheltered too much growing up, she might not even understand how weird people can be. This promotes a situation where weird becomes different, and different, when you are a teenager beginning to explore all that life has to offer, is interesting.

In the interests of not having to scare the crap out of your daughter with explanations of how killers and rapists can lurk inside the most harmless-looking people she encounters, I suggest you ask questions before your daughter starts dating about what she thinks bad people look like, and let her answers steer the conversation. She might surprise you and say, "He could be the guy next door, Daddy. I'm careful to continually assess and reassess everyone I deal with. Whether I interact with a person superficially or on a regular basis, no one is above or below careful, ongoing, and dynamic scrutiny." She may already know that the boogeyman never looks the way you expect him to look.

This response would certainly be better than, "What do you mean, Papa Bear? There aren't any bad people in the world. Everyone I meet is a nice person. I haven't met anyone who *isn't* my best friend after a minute or two."

Unfortunately, there are people who truly believe that nothing bad could ever happen to them, and certainly nothing bad could ever happen to them at the hands of someone they know and care about.

Whether you have carefully exposed your daughter to the potential of evildoing in the world, or not, we must as fathers take it upon ourselves to provide specific examples and guidelines on what our young ladies should be on the lookout for. What signs indicate her potential dreamboat is a long-term train wreck? I know we would all like to be the dad who kicks the ass of every guy who hurts our little angel's feelings. I know I've given some thoughts to how and when this might occur. Unfortunately, if something beyond hurt feelings really does occur, the last thing she needs is you going off and beating the crap out of her assailant in an attempt to make amends for the hurt. It is substantially easier to warn her ahead of time about what sorts of personality issues she's going to face out there, and have her prescreen out the losers ahead of time.

Your mission, should you choose to accept it, is to make her aware of the high-risk personality types out there looking for potential victims. As with all things, there are various grades of bad—from neurotics to control freaks, all the way up to complete sociopaths. You would think that it would be easy to spot the more advanced nut jobs out there. However, if she isn't aware that they exist, she's not going to be on the lookout. The real problem is that a true sociopath is very good at blending in and playing the game. He's not unlike a spy working behind enemy lines. He's learned how to appear normal and not stand out or draw undue attention to himself. He's also likely a master manipulator and liar with compulsive outbursts, ones that may (or may not) have resulted in a criminal record.

As I reminded the retired cop we discussed in Chapter Five, there are many criminals out there who haven't been caught yet. Even if I had the ability to run a criminal background check on a potential boyfriend, it would be just one more tool in my tool kit. I would still want to practice all the skills I shared with you in this book for reading, assessing, and interviewing him. A clean background reveals only that he hasn't been successfully prosecuted yet. There is a world of a difference between judicial innocence and not having committed the crime. There could be a multitude of pets and small animals who would love to be heard from.

The American Psychiatric Association has a laundry list of mental disorders, and tests for discovering and classifying mental health issues. As with all things mental health, the arguments for and against various tests, reports, findings, research, and subsequent data conclusions cover a myriad of potential symptoms or behaviors. However, despite the significance of the work, mental health professionals are some of the most underappreciated and overlooked folks around. Imagine being the person tasked with getting to the bottom of your odd proclivities. Scary, isn't it? Fortunately for you, you aren't the one about to be screened by a very suspicious parent.

In order to simplify what sorts of behaviors you are going to be looking for and discussing with your daughter, I'm going to focus on the dark triad of personality disorders:

1. Narcissism
2. Machiavellianism
3. Psychopathy

When I began researching various psychological problems, it meant a four-hour trip to the reference department of my local library. These days you can at least begin your research on any topic right at home via Wikipedia. Sometimes you'll come across articles that need attention or cross-referencing and you'll need to spend some of your hard-earned moola to dig out the facts for yourself. But the web is a great place to start and at least narrow down the books you'll need, without having to slog your way through hundreds of manuals at your library.

A narcissist is someone who suffers from excessive egotism, vanity, pride, selfishness, and massive amounts of self-love/self-respect. Some self-love/self-respect is healthy; in fact, you want to have a moderate amount of it. (No, not the sort of self-love that requires a wet wipe when you are done.) Self-love/self-respect stops you from having conversations in your head that always conclude with you referring to yourself in a negative way. And please don't pretend that you don't have conversations with yourself when you're alone—no one will believe you. What you say to yourself during your alone time says a lot about your mental well-being. I spent a good part of my earlier life using negative references when pushing myself to achieve things. Rarely would I use positive language to encourage success. When I was going through Commando training it was always things like, "You pussy—suck it the fuck up and keep going," or, "What the fuck is wrong with you, this isn't anything compared to what happened when you were a kid." Or another: "You asswipe (one of my dad's favorite sayings), is that all you've got?" You get the point.

You might be amazed to find out more about yourself once you begin digging into some of the dark-triad characteristics. Don't worry, you can use research into your daughter's boyfriend as a cover for your own journey of self-discovery.

Narcissistic self-love is what is problematic. I mean the sort of self-adoration that results in everyone else coming in a distant third place for anything of importance—yes, you have first *and* second—and this is a best-case scenario. David Thomas, author of *Narcissism: Behind the Mask*, lists the following traits as potential behaviors of narcissists:

1. Arrogant body language, looking down the nose, contempt
2. Problems sustaining satisfying relationships, because it's always about them
3. Lack of psychological awareness; they don't even know they have a problem
4. Hypersensitivity to insults, real or imagined
5. Difficulty with empathy
6. Bragging or exaggerating achievements or capabilities
7. Denial of remorse or gratitude

If Junior shows up for his meeting with you and displays cocky or arrogant behavior, the problem could run deeper than merely false bravado. We all know that a certain amount of confidence and self-assurance can be attractive to the opposite sex. What your daughter needs to know is that if he seems *too* full of himself, she will need to run through problems she may have noticed but not thought much about. For example, if he has had a string of other girlfriends who have all split after a short time and have the same complaints, it was probably him—not them.

You could advise your daughter by sharing stories about some of the people you've dealt with over your lifetime who were a nightmare, from bosses to friends and girlfriends. Anyone who was a complete asshole, but was seemingly oblivious to his or her shortfalls would make a great example. Narcissists come in all sizes, ranging from a minor irritant to a major pain in the ass. He might be subclinical or borderline, wherein no actual diagnosis of Narcissistic Personality Disorder has been awarded, and has never been diagnosed. Individuals with this disorder rarely seek treatment because they don't think they have a problem. But it is only a matter of time before it shows. He also might be pathological, in which case the best place for him is inside a soundproof padded room. Or he might be somewhere in between all of these. We shall all keep our fingers crossed that our girls don't fall for any of these guys, but if they do, that he is on the lower end of the arse-ache spectrum.

Because of a narcissist's sensitivity to insults, if your daughter has a great sense of humor, she could potentially weed out the majority of high-risk love interests simply by poking fun at them. If during the initial courtship, she throws some funnies his way and he reacts poorly, get her to hang a wooden placard around his neck reading, "Here's your sign," so all will know who he really is. The male ego is fragile enough; she doesn't need to get tangled up with a guy who is even more sensitive than most. Come to think of it, forget the placard thing—it would probably make him postal. It would be best for her to back away slowly and let some other poor girl figure him out.

In long-term relationships, and life, someone who lacks empathy is a cold-ass fish. Usually this trait is associated with a guy who cannot relate well to others. During discussions in which an alternative argument is presented, he will likely resort to insults or anger as a basis for dismissing the opposing point of view. He won't even make an attempt to understand what the other person is saying or why he's saying it. The other person's point will be dismissed before a discussion can be had. Normal people will at least hear another person out before disregarding the person's point of view. They will listen long enough to be sure the other person really is an idiot before blocking their ears. A narcissist won't even provide this short grace period. He will also interrupt a great deal, as he will consider his own opinion much more important than other people's opinions.

The individual who brags about his achievements or exaggerates his capabilities is someone we tend to encounter later in life, as adults. As Junior probably hasn't lived long enough to accumulate a wall of accolades, it's going to be hard for him to claim he's already climbed Everest. He may have flown past it, but that's marginally different than climbing it. Even a pronounced narcissist is going to know this. However, he might stretch the truth, exceptionally glorifying his experiences, or even exchanging himself for a person who really achieved the object of the story. He could also just make something up entirely.

Not exaggerating one's experiences or capabilities is tough for teenage boys. Testosterone courses through their blood, leaving them feeling bulletproof. Even if a teenage boy hasn't done what he says he's done, feeling indestructible makes him feel as if he could do it if he had the chance. Not surprisingly, this results in him feeling as if saying he could do anything isn't too much of a stretch. It's the same type of "I can conquer anything" thinking that could drive a former dancer (me) to enlist in one of the toughest military branches in the British Armed Forces, and make it. Insanity comes in all forms.

The narcissist might proclaim he can fix this, endure that, master such and such, and deliver it all without humility or real comprehension of what he's saying. You might feel like losing it, laughing at the absurdity or immaturity of the statement if Junior makes an over-the-top proclamation—but you should try to hold it in.

I was once fortunate enough to film promotional footage for a show idea that my wife and I had. A part of the taping was going to include me sparring with former UFC heavyweight champion Shane Carwin. During the days before we went to Denver to film, I showed my kids some footage from Carwin's Mixed Martial Arts (MMA) fights. I jokingly told them not to worry, as I would do my best not to hurt him during our taping, and we all laughed. A narcissist wouldn't laugh at this. He'd be offended that you don't think he'd be capable of such a feat.

Before actually getting into the Octagon with Shane, I remember telling him, "I've never sparred with a girl of your size, but I'll take it easy on you if you want me to." Oh no, that's right, that's what *he* said to *me* before turning me upside down and dropping me on my head—not an easy feat when the opponent is a piece of British beef weighing in at more than two hundred pounds. The next week was spent applying one ice pack after another to my neck, legs, and ego. Not necessarily in that order. He is a beast, and I most certainly felt my age after my "light" sparring with the former champ. I'm just glad he had a good sense of humor and decided not to crush me simply because he could. Obviously Shane isn't a narcissist or he might not have had enough empathy to see things from where I was standing.

If the young man your daughter brings home begins spinning yarn after yarn, all extolling his exploits and heroics, it'll be an easy ping to call him on it. In the day of electronic everything, most things that are accomplished, if they have merit, can be found online with minimal fuss. Whether you call him on it while he's standing right there in your kitchen, or if you opt to Google-search it after he leaves, will probably depend on the scale of the story he told you. If he already spouted the tale to your daughter and she is aware of what this sort of thing can signify, she may well have done her own search and ruled him out for an introduction to you. This is just one more reason to keep your daughter in the loop and up to date with your findings. The two of you working toward the same objective and playing off the same guidelines and understandings provide her with the best chance of skipping a complete nugget.

The signs that a person is devoid of the ability to feel gratitude tend to show themselves later on in a relationship. But if for some reason you have to do something nice for him before you've had time to assess him, and he isn't very grateful, you're likely going to blow a gasket well in advance of him becoming a long-term fixture in your daughter's life. A lack of gratitude is indicative of feelings of entitlement. He might feel that whatever is done or provided for him is done because of his importance. This is an extension of a narcissistic, superior attitude. When one feels bigger/better/richer/stronger than others, servitude seems like it should be automatic. The "little people" should know their places and act accordingly. This also bleeds over into a lack of humor, at least in regard to himself. It's difficult to find humor at one's own expense when the joke was made by one of the minions who should serve him.

A lack of remorse is also something that is more likely to occur later in the relationship. A lack of remorse typically begins with blaming someone else for something bad that's happened, rather than taking responsibility for one's own causation of it. A remark as simple as, "Sorry, I really messed up," will rarely, if ever, be uttered by a narcissist.

I'm in favor of my daughters being friends with boys they like before they begin dating them. I hope you feel the same way. This should allow your daughter to note a potential boyfriend's levels of—or lack of—empathy, sympathy, loyalty, and, above all, responsibility and gratitude before she gets into a relationship with him. The exception to this is Acquired Situational

Narcissism, wherein the individual begins displaying narcissistic tendencies only later in life. This is usually brought on by wealth or fame, and is a result of feeling superior toward those who lack these things. It takes a grounded individual to not let the trappings of wealth and fame change who he is. As most people like this tend to be surrounded by people who answer to them, honest feedback is not something they are used to hearing. In these situations, anything the narcissist says is right and/or funny, and never contradicted.

When you consider how our society turns ordinary people into superstars at the drop of a social media/reality TV hat, the development and growth of narcissistic tendencies isn't too surprising. Our children are inundated with information telling them that shitty behavior is perfectly okay, so long as the doer of the deeds is famous—for one reason or another. If your daughter understands that most of the "role models" of modern society are damaged individuals, it may help her keep perspective on life. If possible, don't ever miss an opportunity to talk with her about something that might be gracing mainstreet media reports, especially as it pertains to female role models. If an overpaid female singer begins cavorting around onstage and dry-humping a foam finger, it may be a great time for you to ask your daughter what she thinks of such behavior. Don't launch into some long-winded tirade until after you've established how she views the proceedings, as you may be preaching to the choir, and too much "slutty" behavior bashing will only further ignite her curiosity.

A favorite tactic of mine is to ask my daughters what their opinion about such-and-such antics on TV is, and then to ask them how they would feel if I went onstage and did the same thing—with them sitting in the front row with all their friends.

Sophie always laughs heartily. At age nine and a half, I think it would be nearly impossible to embarrass her. She still thinks all my jokes are funny. However, at age twelve, Cora is another story. Inducing a shade of red rarely seen outside of severe sunburn, my eldest girl believes she would literally die of humiliation. I also make sure to ask them why they think so-and-so is doing what he or she is doing. Invariably, they explain it succinctly, using much the same language as I would have used. What we should try not to do is to ignore what they are witnessing daily on TV or social media, as that wouldn't help anything!

As you might expect, narcissism is the lesser of the dark-triad evils. It can get worse.... Individuals with Machiavellian traits are likely to lie and manipulate their way through life, with an attitude that an end always justifies the means. While a narcissist makes life hard on a partner because he loves himself more than anything else in the world, Machiavellians feel very few emotions at all, and as such can completely detach themselves from their actions and the people those actions will hurt.

There are tests (Mach IV and Mach V) used by psychiatrists to help determine if an individual has a high level of Machiavellian characteristics, but unless you are going to insist every boyfriend sit through one, you are going to be on your own in determining whether Junior falls into this category. However, with some clever and careful questioning, you might illuminate potential problems, no written test needed.

Two statements Machiavellians struggle to agree with are:

1. Most people are basically good and kind.
2. Most people who get ahead in the world lead clean, moral lives.

If you ask the boyfriend whether he agrees with these and he rolls his eyes like "How could anyone think those sorts of people exist?" it's because he knows the levels of manipulation and deceit that exist, and he's tried them all! It's going to be challenging for him to agree with the statement that most people are good and kind when he is out there tricking and deceiving his way through life. He thinks that to get ahead, you can't lead a clean, moral life!

It is worth mentioning that most adults would also have a hard time agreeing with these statements. Our excuse is age and wisdom. The older we get, the more we have seen what people are capable of, and thus it is our wisdom and knowledge that would guide us to declare we strongly disagree. We have had to witness and possibly deal with this sort of behavior and have become bitter and twisted because of it. We also develop a wicked sense of humor as a coping mechanism. You can disagree with me if you like, but I won't be listening to your point of view.

If during your time baselining the boyfriend, he's answered simple, open-ended questions with timely, non-stilted replies, and then you ask something along the lines of "You seem like a really nice guy. Do you think that most people are basically good and kind?" and his jaw starts flapping like a fish out of water, then you might have manipulated him into revealing his true colors. Don't feel bad if this happens. He isn't old enough to be as bitter and twisted as we are, and should have youthful optimism on his side, in buckets. Only if he happens to have suffered through some horrendous childhood challenges at the hands of other people might his skepticism be acceptable.

One of the following responses would also be a warning sign:

"Possibly."

"Err, maybe."

"Not sure about that."

"Hell no, ya damn hippy—of course, they ain't!"

It's possible that you will see one or two, or even a variety of nonverbal indicators of discomfort, accompany these responses. Maybe a flash of surprise (eyebrows blasting up into the middle of his forehead), fear (lips drawn back at the corners of the mouth), gestural retreat (backing away from you slightly or in a very pronounced way), stuffing of hands into pockets (hiding what he might really be thinking), chin lowering (feeling vulnerable), emblematic confusion (headshake no when he is telling you yes), adapter (hands covering and moving to protect his nuts), or stance change (feet drawing closer together). If he does all of these, he's going to look like a 1980s break-dancer, and you should most assuredly get the clues.

In addition to having problems agreeing (strongly or otherwise) with either of the two above statements, Machiavellians tend to *strongly agree* with the following:

1. Never tell anyone the real reason you did something unless it is useful to do so.
2. The best way to handle people is to tell them what they want to hear.

However you choose to deliver either of these statements, leave the language as intact as you can. The reference to handling people in question two is amazing. It implies that all people need to be manipulated or placated in some way. In the case of you dealing with the boyfriend, it is correct. Once again, it will help if you ensure your question is delivered as neutrally and void of attitude as possible. Few people will answer questions honestly if they think the person receiving the information is judging them. To keep the interviewee calm, you should agree with whatever he says, keep nodding, and encourage him to explain and expand more. Remember that the more he talks, the more information you can collect. If that means you need to throw in a suggestion or example of your own to make him feel like he's chatting with someone from his twisted universe, then get to it.

I watched a TV show a few days ago that followed some detectives during their investigation into a shooting outside a nightclub in New York City. They had their chief suspect in for questioning, and as one might expect, they were angry that the asshole had opened fire outside a club, killing a bunch of innocent bystanders. But instead of leaving their emotions at the door and entering into what I like to call the emotion-neutral zone, they brought their animosity into the interrogation room, immediately putting the suspect on the defensive. They used language describing how five "innocent" people had been shot and that he was "going down" for a long time, possibly even getting the death penalty. WTF? The last thing you want to do is keep reinforcing the severity of the crime. His body and verbal language told them on several occasions that he knew more than he was letting on, and they needed his confession, but they still attacked him every time he seemed close to possibly sharing damning information. What they needed to do was observe and listen, even if that meant faking empathy or understanding, and use that information to cultivate a conversation.

I recommend that you take one of the Mach tests yourself, answering the questions honestly. This shouldn't be a problem, as you aren't going to have to share any of the information with anyone unless you want to. If you score highly on the test for certain less-favorable characteristics, remember that it's never too late to change... or get therapy. Knowing the results of your Mach test provides clues to how you might exhibit body language signals toward others, either positive or negative. If Junior shows up displaying perfectly normal behavior, but you are all twisted, it won't matter what you think you see. Your own issues will cloud the interview.

Machiavellians also tend to jump from one date to another. They are driven by immediate gratification (and excitement) of new conquests instead of long-term dating stability. Of course, this sort of behavior could be applied to nearly every teenage boy on the planet.... Before writing this book, I took the Mach IV test (you'll be pleased to know that I scored very low—or at least that's my story and I'm sticking with it), but you'd never have guessed that if you reviewed my dating life as a teenager. Much of the current research into Machiavellian behavior has been gathered from college students, and it's difficult to identify behaviors specific to Mach types that couldn't also be attributed to high-strung young adults breaking free of the constraints of living at home for the first time. Other behaviors include impulsivity, substance abuse, many sexual partners, and lower standards in short-term mates. The last habit bodes well for dads of upstanding young ladies, as Machs don't typically aim very high on the dating pool ladder. And now that I've given you a sliver of hope, I'm afraid I must plunge you back into darkness. If he is a good-looking bugger and a master manipulator (chameleon), he's probably considered quite the catch. He knows what to say and how to say it in order to achieve his objective, and is always seeking to further his own agenda at any cost.

If your daughter brings home the class's debate champion with aspirations to change the world through "good deeds" and it all sounds too good to be true, find out how many girls he's already blessed with good deeds. Then see what he thinks of those who have gone before him—"others" who've led the world and been successful. If he makes it clear that he thinks those people did anything and everything necessary to be successful, you'll have a much clearer idea about his true character, and you should go ahead and beat him with the largest stick available! You may never get another chance.

In the media, it first became popular to talk about psychopaths, then sociopaths, and now Antisocial Personality Disorder is the term du jour. There are a range of beliefs regarding what circumstances mold the personality of someone so that these titles fit, from early environmental considerations, to biological or chemical imbalances, to social factors. To the laymen, it all means the same thing: another type of nut job we have to be on the lookout for when our daughters start dating. For ease of clarity, I am going to lump all three of these mental conditions together under one title: psychopaths. I do this because I've watched too many horror movies and can't help but label all evildoers this way. Psychopaths are the worst of the Dark Trio, and the severity of not identifying one could be monstrously serious. This guy is like a narcissist-and-Mach combo on steroids.

You might think that with such pronounced issues, psychopaths would be easy to identify, but they aren't. One of the reasons they can be so hard to spot is that they often function quite well in society, pretending to be one of us "normal" folks. Beyond being thrill seekers, they feel very few, if any, emotions, and see the rest of us as pawns to be used and discarded. As with the Machiavellian personality type, they will charm and scheme their way into the hearts and minds of those around them; but they'll go even further, using our empathy or sympathy against us if it fits their agenda.

It is frightening to think that our daughters may be smart, confident, feisty, independent girls, perfectly capable of taking care of themselves under nearly every circumstance, and yet these guys could still seduce them. How do you teach your daughter to be wary of someone who uses empathy or sympathy as a weapon? In *The Sociopath Next Door*, Dr. Martha Stout, a clinical psychologist, reveals that one of the most popular tools in the sociopath's arsenal is pity. This means that a psychopath might use your daughter's humanity against her. If she finds herself being drawn into a position of doing something because he has manipulated her into feeling guilty enough to go along with the idea, that is her warning sign! Feelings of guilt, sympathy, or empathy are not good reasons to embark on a relationship.

Psychopaths also display poor impulse control, vast depths of selfishness, and an inability to take responsibility for their mistakes. This results in their allocating blame anywhere or everywhere, except at themselves. Their ability to do this is aided by the fact that they feel no shame, remorse, or guilt. They have a "so what" attitude about everything they do, and can never understand why another person is upset. The scale of a hurt they inflict or crime they commit will not matter to them. They just don't care. This makes them impossible to be around for any length of time. It will serve your daughter well to understand that if for some reason she is friends with someone like this, this is not just a phase the person is going through—this defines who they are. So if she has a male friend who has exhibited this type of behavior and the guy suddenly begins applying liberal amounts of charm in your daughter's direction, he's only pretending to care. And he will not make a good pet project—she will never be able to change him! She should not go into a relationship with him based on who she thinks he could be. Her decision should be based on how he acted before the buttering up and showering of attention. It's all too easy for someone like this to temporarily "change" who he is into the version most likely to succeed in conning a potential victim. He will have done his homework to know what he thinks your daughter likes in a guy. She needs to know what his play might be to trick her, and react when it happens. Knowing why he may have miraculously turned a new leaf (yes, I'm laughing out loud) gives her the information she'll need to remain impervious to his lascivious charms.

Our visiting psychopath is also a risk taker. In the face of danger or circumstances that would elicit fear in normal folks, this guy will be as cool as a cucumber. That's because there's a good chance that, alongside missing other normal emotions, he is fearless. Meeting you should make any young tyke at least slightly apprehensive. A lack of nerves could be indicative that he is lacking emotions. I ask you now, would you have believed a girlfriend if she'd told you there was absolutely nothing to worry about before you met her dad? Or would you have been thinking, "I think I'll make that call." Dads can be unpredictable, and just because he may not have killed anyone to-date, doesn't mean he isn't about to start. I don't think there's anything a girlfriend could have said that would have completely assuaged my nerves.

If the boyfriend is all smiles and as relaxed as a bloke can get, it might not be a quiet self-confidence manifesting itself;

it could be that he isn't feeling any normal, anxious emotions. He might even be getting off on this new thrill. The challenge of manipulating and pulling one over on you might be satisfying a deep-rooted urge to trick and connive his way through the interaction. There's a chance he's already anticipating the sense of accomplishment that will follow in conning you into believing he's a nice guy. If you use questions from the Mach tests, at least as a starting point, you can use what he says or how he says it to begin exploring the depths of his depravity. It might be that he doesn't say or do what is expected or normal, and the missing normalcy in either category can lead you down into the rabbit hole that is his mind.

He might display unexpected behavior in reaction to the question, "Do you think most people who get ahead lead good, moral lives?" It might be anger or contempt toward your implied naivete, or no reaction at all. If someone were to ask you this question seemingly out of left field, what do you think your reaction might be? I'd probably be surprised, and certainly taken aback. I'd be thinking, "What the hell is the honest or right answer to that question?" I might also feel apprehension as it dawned on me that this wasn't going to be a normal meet and greet. If you ask these questions, the boyfriend might try to answer "correctly," but if his honest response and perceived correct response aren't the same, he might trip up and self-censor his response midway through. "Of course good, moral people *don't*...do get ahead." A correction in word choice mid-sentence would indicate that his first response was probably the honest one.

During Scott Peterson's interview with Diane Sawyer, he slipped up when referring to his wife, Laci Peterson, by saying, "She was amazing. Is amazing." He quickly added the present

what they should be, the sooner she can work on her exit strategy. Many women caught in bad relationships wait too long before doing what they know must be done—either out of fear, or a lack of grasping just how bad things could get if they don't break it off. Unfortunately, it could get really bad even after a woman does end it. Psycho (or sociopath or Antisocial Personality Disorder) is a term tossed around with casual abandon; but a "horror movie" psycho is what she might get if she isn't able to recognize signs and escape the relationship sooner rather than later. Machiavelli said, "The wise man does at once what the fool does finally," but that doesn't mean the action is easy. Women or girls who have been taken in by and then leave a manipulative S.O.B. are at risk of being seriously hurt or killed after the parting. Restraining orders may even ignite the person's rage further, so her fears are well founded. This is why it is so important for your daughter to understand what characteristics to be on the lookout for in the early stages.

All this talk about psychos and sociopaths isn't all bad news.... No, really! We have all encountered these types and probably didn't even know it. Some function harmoniously with our society and even rise to its upper echelons. They can be doctors, lawyers, or heads of corporations, or even members of the government, military, or police force. What aids their becoming managers or superiors within these organizations are their cold and calculating minds. Void of those cumbersome emotions the rest of us suffer from, they make decisions based purely on the merits of the challenge. They are like Mr. Spock from *Star Trek*, cold, logical, calculating, and dispassionate. Even if an obstacle involves people and feelings, everyone is expendable to them. In my opinion, even though they may climb the managerial ladder, they make terrible leaders. The nuances of effective leadership are beyond their comprehension, as there are too many emotional nuances for these types of people to be truly inspirational.

On the bright side, if she doesn't bring home a pre-med or pre-law boyfriend, and instead you find yourself meeting Billy the trash man, but Billy doesn't display any of the characteristics of a psychopath, he isn't such a bad catch.

Having said all of this, remember that I am discussing worst-case scenarios. Your daughter is unlikely to bring home someone with one of these personality disorders—unless you've done something to deserve it. The next two chapters will look at things he might say during your questioning, and why you'll need to master listening, in addition to observing, categorizing, and planning your follow-up questions on the fly. There are some things I've included that he is probably never going to say, but I always look for worst-case possibilities, and as a dad, so should you! When it comes to building the kind of rapport we discussed in Chapter Two, if you've done a great job until now, then that effort is about to pay off. Asking him smart, probing questions could result in him telling you much more than he intended to, thus arming you with the sort of information critical to helping you decide if he's a winner—or not.

CHAPTER EIGHT

What Is Said

> "It's better to keep one's mouth shut and be thought a fool than to open it and resolve all doubt."
>
> —Abraham Lincoln

No matter what personality your daughter's boyfriend possesses, one thing is for sure: he will know he needs to show up to his meeting with you and be on his best behavior—and this requires being social. He might not intend to say much (or as much as he might actually reveal), or he may intend to bowl you over with enthusiasm and showcase all of his amazing attributes.

We all know how to put on a facade—it's part of playing the "game of life." The degree to which we need to mask our true selves or act in a socially acceptable way depends on who we are and the circumstances we find ourselves in. When it is time for him to meet you, this task can become extremely complicated, potentially for both of you.

If you haven't put in the time practicing the skills you need to read him as accurately as possible, you could miss a sign providing a glimpse of what is behind his polite facade. Reading someone is a perishable skill requiring many months (or more likely years) of practice in order to become proficient.

Depending on how old your daughter is now, you may need to begin cramming and crash studying, or can take your time mastering how to read nonverbal and verbal behavior over the next couple of years.

If you master the skills I've laid out for you, then even if the boyfriend is excellent at hiding his emotions, he's not going to be fast enough to mask, camouflage, and screen what his body and words communicate. He'll have come to the wrong house if his plan was to do this and do it effectively.

In this chapter we'll review how to read his verbal communication, and look at examples of what you can say to guide him toward revealing more than he might want to share. Sometimes what is said and how it is said, or even what is not said, can tell you far more than the speaker intended to share.

In Chapter Four, we touched on how volume can be used as a tool for spatial domination. The chances that he comes into your home being loud and obnoxious are slim, unless he has some sort of hearing impairment. Be careful to make sure this isn't the case before using pepper spray to quiet him down. We interpret what is said in four main ways: one's choice of words, the tone/volume with which they are delivered, the speed and cadence of delivery, and the pauses or fillers used to pervade any silence or awkward gaps. You will want to pay attention to them all, but particularly to tone and volume; this alone could provide insight into what is going on in his head.

We all use volume and tone to provide meaning or emphasis to our words, but we usually do it subconsciously. You would never needlessly shout at a sick person or go higher in pitch when asking how someone is at a loved one's funeral. Your brain knows what is appropriate for certain circumstances and what isn't, and your vocal cords act accordingly.

Junior's tone and volume will relate to the subject matter being discussed. If he is telling you about something exciting that happened, you can expect his volume, pitch, and even the speed of his words to increase. But if the exciting story is made up, then his emotional affect displays and an appropriate increase in pitch and volume might be absent. Or maybe the affect displays are faked, but the pitch doesn't match his face. If his volume and pitch stay consistent from an exciting story through the sharing of a traumatic experience, you might be listening to a tall tale. Our brains are extremely efficient at deciding what volume, pitch, and speed is appropriate to convey the genuine emotions behind our words.

Pauses in speech are a window into the challenges the brain faces when discussing something emotional, taxing, or fabricated. If the brain isn't feeling an emotion, then the body struggles to apply the right gestures and facial expressions to support the words intended to fabricate it. If a person is making up a story, then his brain is working extra hard to find the right words, maintain continuity and sequential logic, and not overcommit with facts that could trip him up later—and do all this while sounding natural. What a challenge! It is during this juggling act that fillers might be used to give the brain time to organize and keep track of all the information. It's no wonder he might begin "umming" and "arring'" his way through a particular topic of conversation. If he isn't experiencing real emotions or recalling factual information, then his brain is working ten times harder than normal to keep everything straight. I wouldn't be surprised if he actually blew steam out of his ears. That would make our lives a lot easier, wouldn't it? Of course, some people habitually "umm, arr, like, you know." If he does this from the outset, then he might not be comfortable conversing beyond his tribe of pot-smoking buddies, and what you are witnessing are his baseline normal communicative skills.

You might not have to ask a plethora of tough questions to get him to trip up. He may back himself into a corner without you having to utilize more than five or six brain cells at a time. If you've managed to build a decent rapport, he is going to be feeling relaxed and ready to share things about himself, and that might be all you need to get the honesty ball rolling.

In a 2002 study by Robert S. Feldman, a psychologist at the University of Massachusetts, it was determined that most people will tell an average of two or three lies within ten minutes of meeting someone new. But why? If you think of how many introductions you've had over the years, you'll probably recall the introductions that were most important, personally or professionally, first. This is because they had the most potential to be consequential to your life. When we are emotionally affected by a new introduction, we become motivated to make a good impression, and this is where problems often begin, especially for men. In the same study, Feldman also discovered that men and women typically tell the same amount of lies. It is the content of those lies that differs. Women will lie to make the other person feel good, while men lie to improve their own image. So a man who feels defensive about his perceived status may agree to take on a project or task that's well above his abilities; he might deny or omit mistakes; or he might start talking out of his ass if that will impress or elevate his status in his listener's eyes. Which of these do you think Junior might succumb to if he has doubts about being good enough to date your princess? Probably all of them! If he has any sense, then he already knows on some level that he will never be good enough. The panic that goes with this knowledge might be enough to make him crazy eager to look good in his stories, even if he has to lie to do so.

There are six ways that someone might lie: omission, commission (making things up completely), embellishing, error, denial, or telling someone else's story. And in order to simplify our task, spotting potential lies, we should use context to guide us to some logical conclusions. We already know that men (or boys) are most likely to embellish facts in order to improve their status. Junior is trying to make the best impression he can. If he's going to err one way or another, it will be in this direction. A rosy coloring of a real event might help him appear more accomplished, at least in his own mind, and you'll need to decide whether to let him get away with it, or cut it down to size once you've realized what's happening.

An error lie is also easily possible. As a young man trying to make a good impression, he might begin talking with you on a topic he knows little about. But instead of admitting this, his jaw keeps flapping way beyond what he really comprehends. This kind of fabrication is ego driven and partly understandable given the context. If you call him out because it's a topic you know a lot about, and he has the fortitude to admit his mistake, depending on what he erroneously claimed, it might also be forgivable. This will depend on how genuinely sorry he seems.

The easiest lies for him to make will be lies of omission. Skipping parts or all information pertinent to a conversation means never having to recant or deny what was said. If he didn't mention it, then it simply slipped his mind. And claiming that something was forgotten is used more than any other excuse when it is time to cover up involvement or knowledge of a crime. The larger the crime, or a person's role in it, the more preposterous this excuse sounds. Unfortunately, in the time frame you have to screen Junior, if he leaves out or stays clear of certain information, there will be little you can do.

When a commission lie is used, the individual has decided to make up an entire story, as opposed to the embellishment approach where there are grains of fact interwoven with the narrative. Commissions are a dangerous endeavor. Details of a made-up story can be difficult to keep up with. He'll find them hard to track, and he's going to have the devil's own time answering even the simplest of questions if this is the route he takes, unless he is pathological! If you get the feeling he's literally making up an entire story, wait until he reaches the end of the diatribe, and then ask him to repeat it, but in reverse chronological order. Even the most seasoned of liars will have trouble recounting a fictional story backward. This is hard enough to do when the details are real, but if a person's made up an event, particularly if he's done it spontaneously, it can prove nearly impossible.

I'd like you to look on the bright side if you do catch him spinning a yarn under one of the following circumstances:

- He omits something because he has a conscience and feels guilty.
- He makes something up, a lie of commission, because he's got imagination and will likely become an outstanding defense attorney.
- He embellishes because he knows he needs improvement and recognizes there's need for growth.
- He lies through error because he's taken a look at your intimidating persona and decided whatever you know, he needs to know—i.e., he's aspiring to be you.

> (Exception: If the schmuck hijacks someone else's story, making it seem like his own, kick the little bastard's ass. That sort of bullshit is unforgivable because not only is he a liar, but he's a thief, too!)

I have a friend who embellishes on a regular basis. His habitual embellishment of facts and details are born of insecurity; so I notice them, but they don't bother me. His wife, on the other hand, often introduces him to new folks by telling them to take anything he says with a grain of salt. And yes, because of this they argue, a lot. If only she would recognize that he just needs his ego stroked every once in a while (and no, that wasn't a metaphor), he probably wouldn't feel quite so inclined to continually stretch the truth.

When it comes to you listening to the boyfriend, and I mean really listening, you have to pay attention to what he *actually* says, not what you *think* he's saying. I know, I'm starting to sound like your wife, but she called me and she had a valid gripe. Men tend to stop listening about halfway through a conversation. It can even happen earlier than that if we think we've already figured out where the topic, point, lesson, etc. is heading. As soon as this occurs, men stop listening and start "fixing." Men begin filling in the information we think we are hearing and blocking out what's actually being said. I'm as guilty of this crime as the next man; but I worked hard on changing, and now I've gone completely the other way. I now pay so much attention to what is being said that my wife would sometimes rather go discount bungee jumping than sit and tell me when something is troubling her.

Junior has a subjective personal dictionary, as we all do. Our personal dictionaries impact the words we use and when we use them. A good example of a change in perception of word choice is a police officer who has to report on the use of his firearm in the application of his duty. He might report the following: "I entered the residence declaring I was a law enforcement officer. The suspect was hiding in a closet and refused to come out. I drew my firearm and approached the closet door. The suspect rushed out at me brandishing a knife. I discharged my weapon to stop the threat." The officer uses "firearm" first, and then switches to "weapon" once he is forced to use it. Until the moment he shoots, it is a firearm. Once discharged, his personal dictionary changes it from a firearm to a weapon. Contextually, this is perfectly normal and understandable. However, if the listener isn't paying careful attention, this change of word choice could be missed, as would the reason for the change. We must not interpret what Junior says while he's speaking, but instead listen to the exact words spoken, and then ask ourselves why he used those particular words. Analyzing words this way, especially on the fly, is harder to do than it might sound. In much the same way as accurate body language interpretation takes time and practice, so, too, does the interpretation of things like word changes, pronoun use or avoidance, past and present tense confusion, and unexpected passivity of language.

I first began researching Specific Content Analyses, the study of what is said and what it might mean, after teaching a body language course to a variety of law enforcement agencies. One of the officers who attended had recently returned from a course taught by Avinoam Sapir, the founder of Scientific Content Analysis (SCAN), a technique for obtaining information and detecting deception. My online research into Avinoam's courses led me to find another instructor of this art,

Mark McClish, and the date for his next seminar was perfectly timed between my travel and presentations. If you are able to attend a Mark McClish seminar, I highly recommend that you do. I've always found learning easier in the classroom (at least since leaving school) with the instructor standing there putting into spoken words (no pun intended) what he means.

So, imagine Junior is standing on your doorstep and this is the first verbal exchange. The boyfriend says, "Hi, nice to meet you, sir." You say, "Nice to meet you, too. Come in." This might sound like a perfectly normal interaction, and it is. We all tend to be a little lazy when it comes to spoken communication, and many things, including greetings, often get shortened. But things aren't clipped only because of laziness. We also shorten our greeting when the enthusiasm isn't really present. "Nice to meet you" is a much weaker greeting than "*It is* (or it's) nice to meet you."

By not owning (and expanding) the greeting, he has already alluded that it might not be that nice to meet you. And who can blame him? In this example, it is his sense of trepidation about this meeting that has squashed any real enthusiasm he might otherwise have felt. This is a simple yet revealing look into Junior's state of mind. Next time you meet someone (other than a new boyfriend), pay attention to your own greeting as well as his. I'll bet that if you're really happy, you'll use a full version; and if you aren't, you'll shorten it. Then he follows that up with "sir." Now don't get me wrong, it isn't that a "sir" isn't nice every once in a while, but delivering a "sir" in this context is self-serving. It is supposed to make us dads feel important and stroke our ego by showing his deference to our position of perceived authority. Know that it's a tool and if you hear it too much, then he's working hard at buttering you up. Cops hear this one a lot, especially when they are interviewing a suspect who is desperately trying to convince them of his innocence. I will say here, though, that if you are a dad who lives in the American South, your job might be a tad more difficult. People there use "sir" as an everyday part of their vernacular, particularly when addressing older citizens. Yes, that's you. You can combat this to a degree by asking him to not call you sir, or instead follow the example below, encouraging him to use your first name.

The tone of the exchange was given a good kick in the balls when Dad replied mirroring the same abbreviated greeting, and then his command for the boyfriend to "come in." As we are interested in developing rapport, consider the following exchange: The boyfriend's opening greeting remains the same, but Dad warms things up by fine-tuning his response with, "Hello, I'm (*first name here*), and it's nice to meet you. Please come on in." Using your first name, rather than introducing yourself as Mr. Whomever will immediately put the two of you on friendly ground, as does asking him to come in with a "please." More on this in a moment.

In the interest of reflecting his language, verbal mirroring, we'll also use his word "nice." We will do this because the subject's personal dictionary is of paramount importance. If he uses a specific word, and the context of your response allows, speak his word back to him. He might consider "nice" to be the epitome of an enthusiastic greeting, or more likely it is his standard social greeting beyond his normal circle of friends. Reflecting his word back helps maintain a sense of balance. If you elevate "nice" to "great" or "fantastic," you run the risk of making him more uncomfortable, rather than more at ease.

Extending an invitation by using "Please come in," rather than a command, lends credence to the expressed sentiment that it really is "nice" to meet him. Expanding "come in" to "come *on* in" will add a small amount of fuzzy and further emphasize that it's an invitation, not a command. We do not command people we like. We treat them warmly with our tone, words, and actions. A corresponding smile and a step away from blocking the entrance will validate the sentiment. His level of anxiety might drop a few points right there. You'll have plenty of time to freak him out a short while later if you need to, but for now, calm words and gestures will weaken his defenses.

His reaction, nonverbally speaking, should match yours. At this point in the proceedings, you haven't given him anything—beyond the fact that the meeting is happening—to be concerned about. So let's look at another possible exchange, still at the front door.

"Hi, I'm here for (*your daughter's name*)." Here's a guy with no intention of hanging around a moment longer than he has to. There's no greeting beyond the bare minimum of "Hi," he doesn't formally introduce himself, and he doesn't even have the sense to pretend he's pleased to meet you. I'm going to go out on a limb here and say he isn't particularly happy about it. It's highly unlikely that he's even put his hand out for you to shake it. He's going to make a break for it the first chance he gets, and not just from you. He's giving you every indication that he intends to make this entire dating episode as casual as possible, and if you could please just get out of the way, that would be great. Chances are that he is expecting your daughter to be dressed and good to go upon his arrival, per his instructions, and any deviation from that plan will cause him agitation.

It's your call, but if a lad behaved this way at my front door, I'd probably tell him my daughter was already out on a date with a *huge dude* who picked her up half an hour ago. Of course, you could also invite him in and try to get to the bottom of things. But it's my opinion that if he thinks he can circumvent the interview with Dad, there are many things he'll try to weasel around, or out of.

Let's say the greeting has gone well and you two are now standing in your kitchen. He is reasonably relaxed and his posture is neutral, with no arms crossed, hands stuffed into pockets, or guarding of the family jewels. You will want to select a few harmless questions to begin gauging his baseline behavior. Notice things like response time, hand and facial gestures, personal dictionary, and anxiety level. Because it's hard enough to baseline someone, I encourage you to break the process down into manageable chunks. Have a list of harmless, easy questions ready to go, and with every third question a curveball. I like this approach because it allows you to measure his responses. They don't all have to sound like ballbusters either. Innocuous inquiries can sometimes work wonders as harmless, yet revealing, probes of attack. Here are a few potential open-ended questions that I might use as my third question, and why:

1. "Where did you come from?" This is a great open-ended question that allows him to share seemingly innocuous information; but it can be interpreted in a variety of ways and his response could illuminate a lot more than where he lives.
2. "How did you find us?" Another seemingly innocent inquiry, but if the little bugger has been to your house before, he might slip up and say it here, while his guard is down.

3. "Nice car. How fast will it go?" Start with an ego stroking statement, then throw the moderate curveball question at him and see how he handles it.
4. "Tell me about a time you've needed to lie." I like this because if he says he's never lied, then you know he's lying—gotcha!
5. "How many are there in your family?" This is not information he should feel defensive about, and it's better than sticking your foot in your mouth by asking about Mom and Dad when he might belong to a traveling circus. A good follow-up to this is, "How do you get along with everyone in your family?"

These questions or variations of them will need to be delivered in a cool, casual manner. While he is talking, you should be nodding, face relaxed with a slight smile. This will encourage him to keep talking and subsequently sharing.

With the first question, "Where did you come from?" it's possible that he will answer with his home's location. If the young stud lives in your town, he'll probably tell you the street he lives on. Or maybe he hasn't lived in the area for long, and so explains where he moved from. More good information. Or lastly, he might have been hanging with a bunch of drunk, drugged-out friends all afternoon, and the guilt he feels about that might cause him to fumble his response. He might say, "Where do I come from? You mean, where do I live? Or where did I come from before here?" Resist the urge to jump in before he's had time to finish. Don't assume you know where he's taking the conversation or his counterquestions. Remember, the more he talks, the better. If the first thing he did was repeat your question back to you, this is a stalling tactic. Repeating the question allows the mind time to formulate the appropriate response—and when I say appropriate, I mean the one least likely to get him in a pinch with you.

As you know, when a subject shares important information, particularly if it is sensitive or incriminating, it is usually the last part of the statement that is most revealing. The last thing he questioned was, "Where did I come from before here?" Dive smoothly into your response to his compound reply and do it from an unthreatening disposition:

"Sure. Tell me where you came from before arriving here." You should chuckle as you deliver your question. Chuckling softens the instruction "tell me," and gives the impression that it never occurred to you to ask where he might have been right before he arrived at your house. Occasionally softening questions stops things from devolving into an interrogation and keeps things on friendly footing. Just don't play it up too much or you'll sound like you've got mad cow disease. If he flashes anger, surprise, or fear, you don't want to be caught up in your chuckling and miss it.

His response, if he is innocent of doing anything untoward before arriving to pick up your daughter, should be fairly quick. A great reply would be, "I was helping my grandmother plant flowers in her garden." If the response sounds more like, "Every Saturday... err, well, today, I was going to go fishing along Muddy Water Springs...," you might have cause for concern. Stating the truth takes little cognitive brainpower. Verbal false starts, pausing like above, and then restarting a statement with something different indicate that a person was going to say one thing, and then changed his mind. Your question then becomes "Why?" What was he going to say?

In the prior example, the first word out of his trapdoor was "every" followed by a day. This signifies that there is probably something he does every Saturday, but doesn't actually want to share with you. He referenced how he "was going to go fishing." This tells you he probably didn't actually go fishing, but wants you to think he did, and then he adds extraneous details about where. If he didn't actually go fishing, then why reveal where it was he didn't visit?

In the case of a verbal false start, chase him up on the reasons he might have started saying one thing and then changed direction. Don't be shy about starting your next line of questioning on that topic—e.g., "What *do* you normally do every Saturday?" Throw him off his game by not focusing on the "story" that he began telling, and most likely will be defensive of, and instead finding out what he normally does on Saturdays, and if there's a good reason he might not want to share it with you.

When you ask this, how does he react? What's his response time? Maybe he replies without pause or concern because he knows his normal Saturday routine won't cause alarm. But what if he says something like, "Normally we hang out at my friend's house to watch the game." This may sound innocuous, but we all know that when groups of men, or in this case boys, get together, trouble is sure to follow. If he says this, there is obviously something about the gathering that caused him consternation—otherwise he wouldn't have verbally started in one direction and then gone off in another. You need to find out what it might be, and not assume you already know. He even gave you information by saying, "watching the game," instead of, "watching a game." Using "the" instead of "a" in an introduction of information indicates he expects you to know which game he is referring to. But never assume anything with him. Hone in on the details of what he reveals and make him commit to something in language. When he's done this, ask your original question again, just slightly differently, "So, is that where you came from today?" This should elicit a clear yes-or-no response. But if he nods, makes an affirmative sound with his throat (mmhmm), but doesn't actually say yes, he is running from committing to a clear answer. Don't let off the pressure, though. He must tell you what it is that is going on, and you must never presume you already know.

At this point, it would be acceptable for you to assume that he watched "the game" today and was drinking during it, but doesn't want to admit this to you before taking your daughter out. This is bad. It could be even worse, though! What if he's a member of a local cult hosting orgies? You and I might think drinking and drugs are bad, but compared to what might really be going on, they're like a trip to Disney World. I know this is all a bit of a stretch, but if he won't tell you exactly what goes on, we cannot be sure. We must never let our own assumptions, internal dictionary, and associated word meanings fill in gaps for him.

In this example, he used the pronoun "we" instead of "I." Because of this, in addition to chasing down what really happens every Saturday and also what he really did today, you will need to find out who "we" is, and what goes on when they are all together. Remember to always ask your questions one at a time. If you throw a bundle of questions at him simultaneously, it is much too easy for him to answer one or two and avoid the tough one. Patience is crucial and patience will be the hardest commodity to come by if you suspect he is hiding something or avoiding giving straight answers. You will also need to fight the urge to rush the inquiries. Take your time, listening to every word of his response, and let his answers guide where you go next. Stay calm, and even play along. I know this is a game with serious consequences, but if you play it right, you might discover more information than you ever thought possible. Play it wrong, and you will get nowhere very slowly.

"That sounds like quite a get-together! How many friends meet?" Ask this question while you are glaring like an enraged bull and he's going to start clamming up, pronto. But deliver the first part of your question as if the activity is the sort of thing you used to do when you were younger, and still wish you were doing, and you'll align yourself with his behavior (and his friends') in a nonjudgmental manner. We never want to presume to be judgmental, at least not until we've squeezed every morsel of truth out of him that we can.

If a time comes when you are suspicious about something you think he may have done, or be intent on doing, quickly figure out the least accusatory language or words possible to describe whatever it is. For instance, if you think he's stealing, refer to the act as "taking." If you think he's aggressive, you might say people "frustrate" him. If he's received twenty-five speeding citations, you could refer to them as "driving awards."

Your only goal is to get to the truth, no matter what that may be. He is much more likely to be honest with you (eventually) if he feels his crimes will be understood. If he feels you aren't about to string him up by his nuts for whatever he's done, he'll be more inclined to share. With a bit of luck, his infractions really will be small and you'll feel better having gotten to the bottom of things. If it turns out to be really bad and he's Jeffrey Dahmer's twin, then keep him talking while you dial 911 and wait for the good guys to arrive. If after you ask him about the "we," his response to your question is "just a few," then he is using minimizing language. When a subject doesn't want to admit facts or the circumstances surrounding an event, one way to avoid guilt and blame is to use minimizing language. Sometimes it can be beneficial as the interrogator to use minimizing language on his behalf. It will be easier for him to come clean about a crime or social infraction if he feels you aren't making a big deal out of whatever it is. If he uses it by his own volition (he isn't just mirroring your language), then he has something to hide. This can extend to details about an incident or the person's part in an action that caused an event.

During the exchange, pay careful attention to any looks of surprise, contempt, or anger. I've watched numerous interviews where the interviewee flashed one of these emotions when it was contrary to the words he was using. In one such interview, the subject flashed surprise when he mentioned his anger toward a person he claimed abused him as a child. Surprise isn't what should have flashed, it just didn't make sense, and it made it clear that he wasn't being honest.

Your daughter's boyfriend might flash surprise at the exact moment he shares more information with you than he intended to, or at how swiftly you are able to hone in on the things he'd rather not talk about. But whether it is surprise or another emotion, if it's unexpected and contrasts with the words said, you don't need to be a mind reader, just ask him about it. Let his words, expressions, and anything that seems out of sync guide your question, then rinse and repeat until you're satisfied that you've reached the crux of the issue, or he's shared everything he has to share. He may well begin displaying irritation or suppressed anger because of the amount of questions you're asking. You'll recognize this if you see a slight frown, a pressing together of the lips, or his hands or frame suddenly stiffen.

If it's only irritation, it won't be very pronounced, but it won't need to be. You'll recognize it because you were already on the lookout for it, expecting it.

Suppose he answers your question about numbers openly, even providing names of friends. If so, congratulations! You'll have a reasonable idea about who was there and can assume that there likely wasn't anything untoward going on. But maybe he stumbles a little over one of the names. This could mean he doesn't get along with someone in the group. If he does, take the opportunity to ask about that person. Once again ask an open-ended question if possible: "How do you get along with (*name-stumble here*)?"

Junior's reply: "Oh, mostly get along fine.... But he can be a bit of a hothead." This reply is exactly the response I received from a friend of mine as we discussed someone we both knew. I just didn't realize my friend knew the individual in question, too. His response lacked any sort of pronoun, e.g., *we* get along. This is a surefire way to create verbal distance from the answer. When someone adds "but," it negates whatever came before it. Like my friend, if Junior adds a "but," he's disqualifying the first part of his answer and they probably fight like cats and dogs. He also used some minimizing language, "a bit of a hothead," to lessen his guilt about ratting his friend out. We can forgive him if it gets us one step closer to the truth.

If in response to this, he pauses a little too long, then it could be that the guy is a flat-out asswipe. For the purposes of this book, I'm always going to err on worst-case scenarios, but the potential exists for the name-stumble to be for completely harmless reasons. I once asked a bloke I was talking to about his siblings, as he had mentioned that he came from a large family. He had two older brothers, one younger brother, and two younger sisters, and he listed them the way you might expect—until he mentioned his youngest sister, whose reference was accompanied by an eyebrow crease displaying mild sadness and a little verbal stumble. I freaked him out a bit when I asked him if she'd been sick recently. It was a lucky guess on my part since it was certainly possible that he was sad for a plethora of other reasons, including her having died. However, it was an educated guess. If she had died, his face would have expressed extreme, not mild, sadness. And most guys are inclined to default to anger if problems surrounding their baby sister involve a human element. Sickness is something even an angry brother can't defend against, so I deduced illness of some sort. For the record, I've made similar guesses in other circumstances and been off the mark, but I don't care about being wrong, as long as I can learn from the errors in perception and become better in the future. You should do the same. Don't be afraid of getting things wrong during your practice times. Go for it, make predictions, voice your observations, and if you're off the mark, so what? Learn, adapt, improve, and go for it again. After my question he performed a slight gestural retreat with his head, raised his eyebrows in surprise, and asked me how I knew that. I didn't want him to be self-conscious, knowing I was reading him, so I sidestepped his question with another: "What's she been dealing with?" I didn't mention illness, I asked a question that could apply to anything from drug addiction to the flu, making it easier for him to discuss whatever it was that she'd been going through—even if it was her own fault.

Turns out that she had broken her collarbone falling off her horse. He had visited her the day before and she was still in a fair amount of discomfort, so his face was congruent with the words he used explaining that he felt sorry for her.

If it turns out that Junior has a valid and reasonable explanation for pausing, stumbling, or looking uncomfortable, then all is well and good. But you will discover that information only by paying attention to clues, and then approaching them in a nonthreatening manner.

When it comes to listing people, places, and things, the order is important. We tend to list information in order of its importance to us, unless the information is harmful. The first person he mentions is probably his closest friend, or at least the individual who impacts him and, potentially, his decisions most. If there is no other indicator that someone in the referenced list of folks is deserving of additional questions, then return to the first name he revealed and ask about that person.

Another tip is that if he mentions a girl first on the list of friends that he "hangs out" with every Saturday afternoon, there is a reason why. The girl might hold special interest for him, or she could have been his best friend since kindergarten, which could make his hanging out with her completely harmless. Either way, it's worth mentioning her name to your daughter so that she may be given an opportunity to pay more attention to their interactions.

Let's look now at the question of "How did you find us?" But before we do, a word of caution: if you haven't been doing a good job communicating with your daughter, or your wife, in regard to the new boyfriend, you might have missed the part where one told you he has been to your house before (maybe with a bunch of her other friends). This is bad for several reasons. First, you are obviously on the outside of the circle of trust. Second, when you jump on him looking like the cat who got the cream for catching him out, you really didn't catch him out on anything. Third, not knowing this important information before meeting him undermines your intention to convey that you have a close relationship with your daughter. You and your daughter must always present a united front if he is to respect your wishes.

If instead of, "How did you find us?" you ask, "Did you have any trouble finding us?" he can answer a simple one-word yes or no. But we want him chattering away like a canary, so give him the opportunity by not asking yes-or-no questions. Chances are that he's going to say, "MapQuest," "GPS," or "I Googled it." There's nothing wrong with a straightforward, honest answer. Not catching him out is a good thing. But if he's caught off guard, he might say something like, "Oh, I've lived around here my whole life." This may seem like an answer, but it isn't. Implied answers like these should raise red flags and motivate you to dig as deep as you can, as quickly as you can, to discover the truth. Your response should be similar to the following: "So, you were already familiar with where (*your daughter's name here*) lives?" or "How many times have you been here before?" With a bit of luck, you'll receive the straight answer you were looking for: "I've never been here before." Or, "I've been here a few times, but you weren't here when I visited." As long as the last answer isn't chaperoned with a shit-eating grin, you are going to have to accept the truthful reply and move on. You may want to hit the ceiling—information like this could ignite the urge—but don't blow the opportunity to discover more about his inner workings. As long as you are prepared to hear a string of honest, albeit potentially unwanted, responses during your time with him, you won't react in a way that is detrimental to the rest of your time together.

What about the following reply: "She must have given me the address." This doesn't mean she actually gave it to him. It shows a lack of commitment; as would, "I guess she gave it to me." If he's guessing the source of the address, so should you. Both of these answers, or ones like them, are also attempts to avoid telling you he's been to your house before. Implied, suggested, or half-answered questions are exactly that, half answered. Don't fill in the blanks for him.

Pray you ask your original question, "How did you find us?" and he responds with something genuine and straightforward: "Your daughter gave me the address with written directions. I don't think she wanted me to be late!" I'm a sucker for a sense of humor, and let's not forget it's entirely possible that this guy is the real deal, a bona fide nice guy. If he uses a little humor, then he is probably relaxed, and this is always a good sign. Humor is also a sign of intelligence. It's tough to be funny when you're a dumbass. And now that I have had my rainbows-and-unicorns moment, let's get back to being serious.

Past, present, and future tenses can be a finicky thing when a statement isn't 100 percent true. Our brains work very quickly. If you recall, an average of four times faster than our mouths. The exception to this rule is the guy your daughter is currently mooning over, in which case the exact opposite is true. Don't feel bad, though. His Justin Bieber haircut is the real reason why she decided this one was a good catch in the first place, and I'm sure her criteria will improve with time.

When we recount a story from memory, all tenses make sense depending on their context, and we use tenses without consciously deciding which one is appropriate. But when part, or all, of a story is made up, our tenses can become awkward because the information is new or "present" to the brain, and is processed at the same time as it's spoken.

In Chapter Five I mentioned an exercise I sometimes have my groups use, wherein they are tasked with writing down three pieces of information about themselves; two are true and one is false. In one seminar I had a detective write down true/false information about himself and then present his statements to the class. After only a few interview questions, he began referring to the wonderful boat trip he had supposedly already taken in the future tense. He had a hard time thinking up something to lie about, so he pretended that the dream trip he planned to go on one day was something that had already occurred. He initially presented his statement in the past tense, as if he had really gone on the vacation. But he lost track of this minor detail as he tried valiantly to control his facial expressions and body language, and the flow of information to the group. During a response to a question about the made-up trip, he changed from using past tense to using future tense. When he was called out on the tense change, he crumbled and began laughing at his mistake. No harm, no foul in this situation, and it helped convey how difficult it is to keep track of everything when you are facing even the simplest of questions.

You might think that asking a bunch of compound questions would make it even harder for the subject to keep things in line. But, as any detective worth his salt will tell you, it actually makes it easier for a suspect to skirt around directly answering parts of the questions he doesn't want to, and/or potentially reacting to all of the information he's trying to keep track of in his head. He'll pick the information he thinks he can most comfortably share, and you'll be stuck trying to figure out whether he has really answered any of your questions honestly. A couple of the detectives in the room knew this and asked singular questions, allowing them to screen and review every response. Each answer received the attention it deserved, and this allowed them to wade through the statements and find the false one.

With your next question to the boyfriend, you are seeking to discover if he is a thrill seeker or hothead. It never hurts to throw a little ego stroke ahead of the main query, so "Nice car.... How fast will it go?" could be great. But if his car is clearly a piece of crap and you already know it couldn't break 55 mph downhill with a tailwind, you'll have to use your imagination and come up with something else to uncover reckless tendencies. On the bright side, at least he won't be driving the rust bucket like a maniac with your daughter inside!

Looking past the ego stroke, let's discuss why I referred to his car as an "it" instead of personalizing his ownership with "your." I could say, "How fast does <u>your</u> car go?" But this would create more of a connection between him and the speed with which the car can go. And what I want to do is provide him with a bit of separation from the responsibility of that speed. Providing him with "distance" between him and his car's performance capabilities is like wrapping him in a warm blanket of insulation. You have allowed him to answer the question without admitting that he has pushed the car to its breaking point. An even worse way to ask would be, "How fast have you driven your car?" If worded like this, he'll have to choose between answering honestly about its performance and needing to lie to create the distance himself. The obvious downside to a situation like this is that he cannot say how fast the car can go without also owning responsibility for that speed. However, if you broach the topic by creating space between him and the vehicle, it will be easier for him to answer. I know this may seem like silly semantics, but you will not believe the power and speed at which this type of questioning can work.

Smart interrogators plan ahead. They know how and where they will begin their probing, employing tactics to make it easier, not harder, for the subject to admit foolishness, association with an event, and even guilt. Know ahead of time what information you want to harvest and the sorts of questions you'll need to ask in order to elicit an honest response. Careful crafting of your questions will result in Junior eagerly admitting to things, and he won't know why or how this honest streak occurred.

As for us, if our daughter changes her boyfriend as often as we change our underwear, then we are going to get plenty of practice honing our questioning skills and choosing our words. So let's review some more possible responses to the question, "How fast does it go?"

1. "I swear to God, sir, I wouldn't know."
2. "No idea."
3. "That used to be my friend's car and it's gone well over 120 mph."
4. "To the best of my knowledge around 75 mph."
5. "Oh, that old car? What makes you think it will do anything above 55 mph?"
6. "I've been immature and reckless and will never do that again! You know when you realize how bad some mistakes are and you learn from them? I'm not planning on being that crazy ever again, sir."
7. "220 mph once I hit the nitro."

You already know how I feel about "sir," and detectives across the world will tell you that once a subject begins swearing to a higher power, then your bullshit meter should go into overdrive. There's something about bringing in an "all-knowing, all-seeing" being that is supposed to convince us they could never tell a lie. You can go ahead and call it horseshit if this happens.

His use of the word "wouldn't" prior to "know" is also a poor choice. It is supposed to imply that he has never gone fast, so he doesn't know what the car's top speed is. But that isn't what he said. He said he wouldn't know, not that he doesn't know. It's more likely that he means he wouldn't want to recall that information right now.

In response number two, he lets you know he's full of doo-doo. First, he doesn't even bother to try to own the response with a first-person pronoun. At least if he said, "I have no idea," he'd be getting behind the statement. Dropping ownership creates as much distance between himself and the remark as possible without just ignoring the question completely. In addition, how often have you really had "no idea" about the capabilities of something you own? Even an idiot has ideas. I have about three hundred a day. And if someone asked me something I wasn't certain of, the least I would do is guess—unless, of course, I knew exactly what the person was talking about and didn't want to go anywhere near responding in case I incriminated myself. If Junior says he has no idea about something, then you've hit a nice tender hotspot and don't stop now, Daddy, let him have it.

Number three begins with the word "that," before continuing with "used to be my friend's car...." In a statement, "that" creates distance between the speaker and the information or declaration. "This" creates closeness or ownership of the statement. For example, "that is a good idea" implies that an idea exists, but the speaker in no way owns it. "This is a good idea" makes it clear that the speaker has carefully thought about the statement and is personally behind it. In this example, he goes on to create even more distance about his knowledge of the car's speed by introducing a third person, particularly one who has the word "owner" in his title. Everything about this statement creates space and separation. Only a guilty person would put this much effort into trying to create a Grand Canyon–sized space between himself and his words.

"It's gone well over 120 mph" is another disowning and separation tactic. "It's" is used to insinuate that the speed the car has gone has nothing to do with its driver. But if the friend had been the one who pushed the car up to 120 mph, then there wouldn't be any need to create additional distance between the speeder and the car. A better close to this statement would be, "And he's taken it up to 120 mph." This would continue allotting responsibility to the friend. By weakening the claim using "it has" instead of "he has," the boyfriend has denied us that connection, and we will want to know why.

"To the best of my knowledge" is intended to imply that he has told us everything, but what it really says is that he has told us as much as he is willing to tell. A statement like this allows the individual to come back later, during additional questioning, and say, "It slipped my mind." The person hasn't quite committed to the line of crap he is trying to feed you with a flat-out, clear-cut testimony such as, "I don't know how fast it goes." That sort of announcement is more likely to be honest. In a statement like that, he is owning it and jumping right in and telling you as much. Simple outbursts with full ownership are harder to come by, at least for the guilty, than you would think. The person doesn't want to paint himself into a corner and have to retract the response later if there is evidence to the contrary. That sort of situation wouldn't sit well in a court of law or with a prospective father-in-law, and he knows it.

"Oh, that old car? What makes you think it will do anything over 55 mph?" This answer gives every indication that the query has been satisfied. But not so quick! Fillers like "oh," "err," "hmm," "like," "kinda," and "you know" are used too often these days to give a speaker time to think and fill dead-air space while he's doing so. Starting a reply with an "Oh" or a similar word is a way to pause, consider the appropriate response, and then reply. In addition to doing this, in this context it suggests that he is surprised that anyone would think about speeding in that old relic. "That old car" insinuates that you must be an idiot to think it could speed. The concluding portion cements the sentiment and encourages you to retract the question because of its lunacy. Answers to questions with questions are always intended to throw off the interrogator by creating doubt about the validity of the question. If he doesn't want to do this, the person will just answer the bloody question. Politicians do this all the time. They throw back questions promoting the viewpoint that they would never do such-and-such a thing because of X, Y, and Z, and what possible reason could they have for doing that bad deed in the first place? They rarely actually answer if they are guilty.

This misdirection tactic is infuriating to watch on television. You see it when some crooked politician wishes that what he said would suffice, but journalists won't let go. He'll throw angry questions out in an attempt to distract people from his not answering. Can you imagine how mad you're going to be if your daughter's new flame thinks he can pull one over on you while he's occupying space in your kitchen?

Your temper will officially and swiftly move to DefCon 226 if this happens—but don't let it show! Stay with your original inquiry until he satisfies you with an honest answer or concedes defeat and leaves.

Answer number five, "I've been immature and reckless and would never do that again. It's like when you realize how bad some mistakes are and you learned from them. I'm just not planning on being that crazy ever again, sir." This answer is a combination of two separate responses given by two different politicians to journalists during press conferences. Sometimes they get away with murder, literally and figuratively, by being very careful about the words they use to dance around delivering straight answers to straight questions. At first glance, the opening of this remark sounds like remorse, maturity, and acceptance to having gone very fast at some point in the past. But is it?

Let's start with what he doesn't say. He doesn't mention what it was that he did that he considers immature or reckless. He also claims he would "never" do "that" again. "That," as you now know, is a distance word; and if the subject doesn't specify what it is he's claiming he will never do again, we can't presume to know what he's referencing. It indicates that whatever it is he did, he'll likely do again, and his subconscious already knows it, thus the lack of verbal ownership.

When someone refers to himself as having been ____________ (fill in the blank with whatever term he uses, in our case "immature"), the listener typically projects a meaning onto the topic at hand. But when it is delivered void of linkage to a particular subject, it could mean anything. He could be referring to smashing his neighbor's windows when he was seven. It is easier to admit to being immature in general terms, as we have all been immature at some point in our lives. The order of the words is also important, as "immature" is closest to the subject-pronoun contraction "I've," and "reckless" is further away. Once more this is indicative of the process of distancing. When a claim is made regarding a particular behavior or mistake, we want to know what the error was.

As always, be mindful of whether his nonverbal signals match his response. If he is telling you how sorry he is or how much he has learned from his mistakes, how does he act? Does he lower his head slightly? Are his eyebrows slightly knitted together, indicating sadness or remorse? Does he give the impression of being regretful about his actions? Assuming he is referring to the specifics of a mistake and his gestures are congruent with the words, then he is probably being honest. But if he skirts the details or doesn't include any, and his body language is out of whack, then he is sending you information all right—just not the sort he intended to.

He then lets you know how much he doesn't own the middle part of his answer by using the pronoun "you" instead of "I." He projects his guilt onto the listener this way, sharing responsibility and tugging on the listener's heartstrings by suggesting we have all done something "bad," and we have all "learned" from it. But if he still doesn't own up to anything, he probably hasn't learned a thing. By using "planning" in the final part of this statement, he insinuates that he won't be as crazy again as he was in the past. I have had plans to go to the moon since I was a kid, but that never happened. Hell, how many plans have you had in your life that never came to fruition? We plan things all the time, but plans change. That's the problem with closing language like this. It says little of real substance, and yet words are leaving his mouth at a rate of knots. Not only did he not answer your bloody question, but he insulted you with a "sir" to round it off.

The last response of "220 mph once I hit the nitro" leaves nothing to the imagination—but at least it's honest. It also signals that he is as dumb as a fencepost for sharing that sort of information with his girlfriend's father. It's okay at this point to offer to show him where a good-sized canister of nitro can be inserted, before you kick him out.

"Tell me about a time you've needed to lie." This is a bugger of a question for him to answer, as there really isn't a good response. A variation is, "Have you ever told a lie?" In the first example you provide him with an escape route by suggesting if he did lie, it wasn't totally his fault—he "needed" to lie. This encourages him to come clean, confess, and use the bait you provided as an excuse. He has a lot less maneuvering room with the other version of the question. As we know, everyone at some point has lied, including Junior, so he can't honestly claim to have never done so—at least not without us laughing at him. So the point of this question is to see if he has a conscience. If he looks suitably chastened as he explains, "I felt I had to tell my mom her hair looked great with her awful new highlights because I didn't want to hurt her feelings, and I really regret doing it," then awesome. But if he says, "I have to lie to my parole officer all the time, otherwise I can't leave the state," and there isn't a hint of guilt or remorse, Captain Obvious says you've got a problem.

A nice final question revolves around his home life: "How many are there in your family?" What you really want to know is if they are still around or if he has their heads in a chest freezer back on the family farm. If they still have pulses, what is his relationship with them like? Does he talk lovingly about everyone except his dad, at which time a facial tick registering 8.9 on the Richter scale launches under his left eye? Listen for distancing language, signs of discomfort, facial incongruences that don't match his words, or hesitancy to expand and elaborate. If he spouts one warm fuzzy story after another (as long as it doesn't sound too good to be true) and answers follow-up questions without demonstrating hesitancy or undue stress, he might hail from a stable, "normal" family background. And you have one more concern to be checked off the worry list.

There are many ways to handle the conversation from here, all of them dependent on his verbal and nonverbal responses. I have given you a few examples of what to ask so the conversation keeps moving, and moving in a manner that is beneficial to you. The first challenge is to come up with good open-ended questions. The best place to start getting a feel for where to begin your interrogation is off information your daughter already knows about him.

The second challenge is going to be to listen like you have never listened before. You are going to have to listen while observing every twitch and nuance of his behavior to ensure that his other forms of communication gel with his words. All of this definitely takes practice, a lot of practice. In addition to the two verbal statement classes (SCAN and Statement Analyses) I recommended you attend earlier in this chapter, I also encourage you to visit www.statement-analysis.blogspot.com to review hundreds of statements and begin getting a feel for how professionals analyze them.

In Chapter Nine, we are going to look at ways you can begin discouraging him from hanging around your daughter if the two of you discover that he is an absolute whack job.

I know it's unlikely that your daughter would bring home someone this bad; but if she does, you are going to want to know how to let him know that he isn't the only crazy in town. And even though this scenario will probably happen to only a few of you, you should all plan for the worst, just in case!

CHAPTER NINE

Dealing with an Asshole

> "It is hard to fight an enemy who has outposts in your head."
>
> —Sally Kempton

We once had neighbors who behaved more like college drunkards than the midthirties parents they were. They had a couple of kids below the age of seven, but that didn't stop them from beginning their drunken street parties around 9 p.m. They would invite a couple other "party-hardiers" on the opposite side of the street and party into the wee hours of the morning. Their antics weren't relegated only to Saturday nights either. They would throw a couple midweek celebrations into the mix just to keep things interesting. After a few weeks of this, it became a nightmare. We would be woken up at all hours of the night and early morning with them shouting, cursing, laughing hysterically, smashing beer bottles, screaming at each other, driving their golf cart across everyone else's garden, and basically doing anything they felt might be funny to them at 2 a.m.

I tried politely to ask them during a couple of their soirées to please keep it down, but it was to no avail. Carol and I both had to work the next day, and had young children trying to sleep, but that didn't mean much to these folks in the middle of another drunken debacle. I concluded that other tactics would be required. As I had no practical way to dispose of the bodies, or any desire to adopt their children after they departed this world, I knew the tactics would need to be subtle, be legal, and carry an impact that would linger in their tiny minds even when drunk.

My plan was to ambush the first one of them I saw outside their home; but instead of approaching full of obvious piss and vinegar, I would utilize the powers of stillness and distance. We'll look at distance in a moment, so first let me share the power of stillness. When someone is mad at another person, he or she often gesticulates aggressively and becomes very animated. An escalation in arm and hand motions goes along with glaring and compressed lips. When two males square off, it is normally an exercise in bluffing. The chest is inflated, the head is reared back, and in true animal fashion, one displays a posture intent on scaring the other protagonist into submission. Fighting is a last resort. It's better to intimidate one's opponent into walking away, and not risk injury to either party (or arrest), than to begin swinging wildly. Your being calm and motionless is the last thing that the other person would expect. When one does not use hand gestures or arm movements, when the head doesn't move and only the eyes travel, and even the blinking is taken down to as infrequent an amount as possible, then things begin to feel very unsettling. The energy around the person limiting his movements becomes predatory, like a big cat coiled up before launching forward and attacking its prey.

One day after another of their drunken night binges had kept us awake until 3 a.m., I arrived home from a trip to the grocery store to find one of the culprits loitering in his driveway, drinking even more beer. One of his children was screaming inside the house, his wife's car was gone, and the other of his young ones was running down the middle of the road wearing a diaper that bounced between his knees. It was so full that the weight of it was dragging it off the poor little guy's backside. Watching, I felt myself becoming angrier by the second; but I committed myself to maintaining calm, and approached him with the aforementioned extreme stillness method, tailored to look menacing. I never swung my arms, but neither were they locked down by my sides. I didn't clench my fists either. He might not have been the sharpest knife in the drawer, but his subconscious would have warned him if they had been squeezed tightly closed, and I didn't want to go into this meeting of the minds putting him into a defensive position, I wanted him unsettled and anxious. My goal was to freak him out to the degree that the next time he was drunk, he would not be able to shake a horrible nagging feeling in the back of his alcohol-addled mind that "wacky psycho guy" (that's me) might appear out of the shadows of the night at any moment. I wanted to make an impact, a creepy, creepy impact.

Understanding and using proxemics, or the concentric rings of personal space expanding outward from each person, can be a powerful tool when used properly. The term "proxemics" was coined by Edward T. Hall in 1963, and refers to the distance around a person. It starts with one's intimate space and moves outward through personal, social, and public distances. When people communicate, they choose a distance from which to exchange words and signals based on their familiarity with each other, their surroundings, and the context of their exchange. The distances more or less break down as follows:

Intimate: Less than 1.5 feet

Personal: 1.5–4 feet

Social: 4–12 feet

Public: 12–25 feet

If two folks are chatting in a crowded room, they'll be within the smaller of the social distances. If those friends are chatting in an open space, they will likely be in the middle of the social-distancing spectrum. If they just met and are in an area with lots of space, the gap between them might be eight feet, unless the person they have just started talking to smells, and then it could be twelve feet, if not farther. Most people would rather shout than breathe in someone else's body odor. I know I would.

If a person (me) desires to speak with another person (my neighbor), and that person is standing in his own driveway, approaching the person to be within twelve feet of him is a risky venture. People can be territorial on their turf. In order to throw off any chance that my noisy neighbor would become aggressive with my intruding into his personal space, I smiled as I invaded straight through his public and social boundaries, until I arrived at the very edge of his personal space. My smile wasn't a true smile, what is scientifically known as the Duchenne smile. My mouth was curled up, but that was as far as it went. My eyes were not crinkled, a sign of happiness. As sometimes happens when someone is disconcerted and unsure what might be about to transpire, my neighbor bore a similar facial expression. The difference between ours was that his came with a slightly nervous undertone and a hint of confusion. As he and I had exchanged pleasantries once or twice before in regard to the noise emanating from his home during the wee hours, he knew I probably wasn't happy about the previous evening's events. But then again, I didn't look particularly upset either. I'm sure he didn't know what to think. In fact, I was counting on that.

I'd selected a relatively neutral stance, with my feet shoulder distance apart and arms hanging relaxed by my sides. However, I'd ventrally oriented myself toward him, rather than moving off to a slight angle. He asked how I was doing, and I answered as quietly as I could while still being audible, "Nicely." That's it. I didn't expand. I didn't change my neutral expression. I didn't move my hands, head, or face. I barely even moved my lips. And I kept quiet.

Silence can be very uncomfortable when it is used the right way—like in this instance. When silence permeates between two people who don't know each other very well, things quickly become uncomfortable. Usually both parties will begin seeking alternative distractions and search for a way to extricate themselves from the awkward situation. The head pivots and the eyes zip side to side in an attempt to find asylum elsewhere. My neighbor's eyes were zipping quite a bit.

Then, because I had answered his question about my day so quietly, he asked me to repeat what I'd said. "I'm sorry, I missed that...." He hadn't missed what I'd said—he just needed more time to figure out what was going on. "Nicely," I said again. Not a thing more. There are many ways to interpret that word, and I watched him flash a moment of surprise when he realized what I'd said. I know he was surprised because it wasn't what he expected to hear. Of all the words he had probably expected me to say, this wasn't one of them. I also tried very hard not to show a genuine smile of pleasure as he began rocking from one foot to the other. I could tell he wasn't sure whether to walk away or to try to find a way to make me loosen up and behave more normally. This was not going to be his lucky day. My time being normal with him had expired weeks ago.

He didn't ask, but I told him anyway, "I've been to the grocery store. Milk is a little cheaper today." You would have thought I'd sprouted a third eye in the middle of my forehead. He couldn't have looked more confused. I still hadn't moved, and I still hadn't spoken much above a whisper. I was more than a little curious what his reaction would be. If he had any sense, he'd have walked away. But it's amazing how a guilty conscience can make someone stay where he is, if only to figure out how bad things are going to get. He launched into a detailed explanation about the fact that his wife was at the store right then, probably getting milk, among other essentials, and that he was going to go with her, but decided at the last minute to stay home and tidy his garage. I received a lot of details about her trip and his garage. People do not like silence.

I decided now was the time to move my head. I tilted it very slowly to one side, looked past his noggin into his garage, and said, "Fun." Then I laughed. Not a particularly hearty laugh, more of a forced oh-my-God-he-must-have-just-been-released-from-the-asylum laugh. It was short and sweet and he mirrored it with a laugh of his own, although I could tell from the confused look on his face that he had no idea why it was funny.

I took a step closer to him. We were now less than three feet apart. He began to pace in a half circle around my front, arms swinging slightly, a sign that his subconscious was readying itself for defense. I was now officially inside his head. He didn't know what the hell was about to happen, but whatever it was, his brain was telling him it didn't look good.

I remained perfectly still, once again. My eyes followed him as he paced, but I moved my head only once he reached the farthest point that my eyes could swivel. Then I would track around to his new position slowly, and once I reached his new position, he would move again. It felt as if I was chasing him around his driveway with nothing more than my eyes. At this point, his guilty conscience got the better of him and he began half apologizing about the previous night: "If they were making noise too late into the evening...." He trailed off without finishing his statement, but I thought his language was interesting. "If" is a weak way to begin an apology (if you could have seen his face you'd have known that was what he was trying to do). It suggests that the potential exists that they weren't doing the described action, and "if" they were, he would have no intention of taking sole responsibility for it. We both knew damn well that he and his cronies were extremely loud. If he didn't think that, it wouldn't have occurred to him to mention it, let alone begin apologizing for it.

He concluded his pathetic apology by referencing "the evening" in an attempt to minimize the late hour of the event. I already knew what he was going to say next, although I didn't expect him to add the last portion: "I was smashed last night, so I have no idea what time of day we were up until."

Oops. Apparently he knew exactly what time of "day" they were up until, as he even politely changed the reference from "last night" to "day" for me. And even as my nervous neighbor claimed to have been too drunk to recall how late they were playing silly buggers, he suggested it was extremely late, as he referred to the current day, and not "last night."

It was then time to play my hand. "I've always wondered what it would be like to wake up and find someone sitting comfortably by my bed in the middle of the night. What about you? You'd be left with that sense of helplessness, certain vulnerability, not knowing how long they'd been there or what they could have done if they'd wanted to." I chuckled at the end of my statement, just enough to imply that I didn't find it scary at all, but rather found it amusing and exciting. My neighbor stopped pacing. He froze.

As soon as the words came out of my mouth, I turned away from him as fast as I could. I literally spun in a tight circle and just caught a glimpse of him jumping about half a step back. He'd mistaken my sudden blast of activity for an attack. I would never recommend turning your back on your antagonist, but I felt reasonably certain that he wasn't about to turn the fearful jump backward into a sudden desire to attack the weirdo.

As I walked away, I kept talking: "The problem with being loud and drunk is you can't possibly hear who's behind you. I would never want to feel that vulnerable."

In the sharing of this, I'm still amazed that he took it all to heart. We didn't hear from him or the other rowdy neighbors again. They were still up until all hours, three or four times a week, that didn't stop; but they never again allowed themselves to reach a volume loud enough to wake me. It was only on the rare occasions that I was up to take a pee that I'd check outside to see what they might be up to. Sure enough, they'd still be up and going strong at one in the morning, but their volume was carefully monitored and none of their usual antics disturbed the peace. It now feels so theatrical to have done this, but at the time I wanted to try this tactic first, before I went postal at 3 a.m. because they had woken us all up again. It worked. Weird and freaky nearly always works because nutty is hard to predict. A little bit of crazy can unsettle even the hardiest of souls, as it speaks to the unleashing of the boogeyman in our most twisted dreams. Horror movies leverage crazy as an excuse for the worst of human depravity, and although you probably won't need to go to horror movie lengths to put the fear of God into Junior, a little bit of crazy might be all you need to inspire him to look for greener, and easier, girlfriends, if you deem him unfit for your daughter.

Of course, if you've taken the time to discuss the kinds of boys she should be steering clear of, then hopefully there's zero chance of a young drunkard ending up in your kitchen. As you will have undoubtedly already explained to her, prescreening her potential dating choices as diligently as possible before becoming involved is always better than trying to find ways to escape him after the fact. It will lower everyone's stress level if she's making decisions about whom she dates based on a list of good options, rather than picking the lesser of the evils.

And speaking of evil, let us pretend that she missed one or two signals highlighting his true colors. If so, don't be mad at your daughter. There are some things she couldn't possibly ask potential dates without seeming like she is pulling double duty as an undercover cop, thereby eliminating herself from the dating pool. And no, I'm not telling you what those questions are. She deserves to at least be out there giving love a chance. But there are things that you can do to begin messing with him if you decide he's a waste of space before they leave on their first date.

Utilizing proxemics is one of them. You can ask the most harmless question in the world, but if you ask it within six inches of his face, things are going to get really uncomfortable. Crowding someone can also be a positive thing. For instance, a good interrogator knows that getting close to a suspect can be used to promote a friendly, supportive tone. If, in the middle of a question, a cop's suspect begins assuming a fetal position, it is not the time to apply more threats; it's the time to comfort the subject and support him if he chooses to come clean about the crime. By lending a sympathetic ear, the suspect feels as if he is quietly confiding in a buddy, rather than helping cement a case against him in a court of law.

This type of approach to the space between the two of you is one way for you to dig deeper into a particular subject without necessarily having to use threats of violence. I know my example of space utilization with the neighbor leaned heavily on intimidation, but this guy had kept me and my family awake at odd hours for weeks. He's lucky I decided to skip plans A and B, and instead go straight to plan C—harmless proxemics with a pinch of crazy. In case you are curious, plan B involved a taser and about a dozen twenty-four-inch zip ties to secure them all in one of their garages. I can't say what plan A was.... I have too many friends who work in law enforcement.

Depending on the boyfriend's age, you might be able to find out more about his temperament from his ex-girlfriends, assuming he is old enough to have had some. Any rumors that your daughter might have heard from the grapevine would be good to know. Because, even though rumors should be taken with a grain of salt, they'll give you potential clues and an avenue of inquiry. If your daughter isn't privy to the rumor mill but is able to provide a name you could pull out and use (if circumstances require it), that's another plus. If you can't gather any of this information, don't sweat it. Even without intelligence of this sort, you can still dig around with questions that imply you know more than you do. Try a comment like this: "Tell me what happened between you and your last girlfriend." If he hesitates or looks like he's seen a ghost, don't jump in and fill in the silence. Let him stew in it for a while.

He might flounder around looking for a good answer, or he might provide an immediate response: "Nothing. I've never dated anyone before." Yeah right! Alternatively, he might fire back, "What did you hear?" or "What do you mean?" or "What are you talking about?"

If he answers your request with a question, don't answer his question. Follow up with a strong suggestion: "In your own words tell me what happened." Wording the suggestion with the phrase "in your own words" insinuates that you already have her words, and now you want his side of the story.

"Tell me" is a command, even when uttered in the soft and caring way you'll deliver it. Hopefully it will prod him into telling you exactly what happened, assuming there's something to tell. The older he is the better the chances are that he has dated plenty of girls before your daughter. Most likely, he won't describe the last amicable breakup he had, because why would you be asking about that? His guilty conscience will do some of the work for you. And if he does spin you that version, but look like a fish out of water before starting, then something doesn't add up. Instead, he'll revisit the one with the most disturbing memories for him. Whether those memories are disturbing because she was loony, or because he was, is what we need to find out. This type of questioning is going to produce a great deal of stress for the young man. If you get the feeling he wants to tell you something but is afraid, move in closer.

It is always easier to confess something quietly. No one wants to shout at the top of his lungs that he has been naughty. This means that you may need to get closer to the little bugger to allow him to whisper what he did wrong. If it seems as if he is a gnat's nut away from sharing something monumental, you might even extend a caring hand placed on the shoulder, in conjunction with the words, "We've all had our share of bad luck. I just want to know your side of things."

This suggests that the circumstances of the breakup were out of his control. Even if he beat his last girlfriend to within an inch of her life, while we are trying to get him to share why he did it, we won't judge. We listen—preferably with a weapon in our back pocket. Of course, until he at least hints at what kind of "bad luck" he endured, it's going to be impossible to know which direction to go in. Stay calm and patient, and coach the confession out of him.

You might need to do more than calmly guide him into talking about it. You might need to play along. Maybe he begins shrugging his shoulders instead of talking. Shrugging is an action we are all familiar with, and it tells that the person is unsure about something. If he does this, he's probably unsure if he wants to tell you he's an asshole who beats his girlfriends. It might be that his last girlfriend beat him! If so, imagine the humiliation he must feel. Information like this would be difficult for any guy to discuss, and although, as dads, it is our prerogative to presume the worst, until we know what troubles the boy, we should play along. Sometimes this means not reacting to information we find humorous because it isn't as bad as we thought it was going to be, and sometimes it means pretending to be something other than what we really are by pretending to understand what made him do whatever it is he did.

If you are standing as close to him as you can without making him all wet behind the ears, start talking blame, and not his. Suggest things like:

"Did you guys argue?"

"Was she difficult to be around?"

"Did she have mood swings?"

Take the conversation in whichever direction you want to take it, so long as your words suggest that whatever caused the breakup wasn't his fault. You are opening the door for him to share with you understandable reasons for why he did what he did. One of the best choices at this time, from his point of view, is a reason why nothing was his fault. If they argued a lot, they share responsibility for the fighting. It will be irrelevant to him that they fought because she was trying to defend herself against his jealous ranting. In sympathizing with him make sure he knows that you think that if she was difficult to be around, then it is not his fault things ended badly.

Whatever you need to say to give him a plausible reason why nothing he went through with the ex-girlfriend was his fault, say it. Be sure your wife and daughter are already aware that if you suddenly start touting the upside of "slapping a bitch" every once in a while, it isn't because you've suddenly lost your mind. It's because you are playing into his sense of entitlement and gently leading him toward a nice, full confession.

You might get lucky. Instead of wasting your time asking a bunch of questions, he might be forward with a comment like, "I would never hit a girl" or "That bitch had it in for me ever since I dumped her for her sister." Unless you use "ever" in your question—for example, "Have you ever hit a girl?"—"never" is not an acceptable substitute for "no" in an open response from the subject. A denial indicating he's been blamed for this sort of thing before would be "I did not," or "I didn't hit/beat/abuse (*the person's name here*)." Consider the athletes who have stood before us to deny they've taken performance-enhancing drugs. How many have said, "I have never used XYZ to get ahead... blah, blah, blah," only to then turn around weeks, months, or in some cases years later to admit they not only used XYZ, but made the rest of the drug alphabet their bitch, too.

What the guy standing in your kitchen is really saying with the statement "I would never hit a girl" is "I would never hit a girl (generalization) who is under my control," or "I would never hit a girl while her large, hairy father is standing watching over us." If his statement was "I didn't hit my old girlfriend," you might be able to believe what he says. If he repeats this declaration repeatedly and uses her actual name instead of referring to her as "old girlfriend," it's even better. We like this sort of statement because he owns it. "I" then "didn't" are followed by a specific reference to the crime and the person it affected most.

Note: Avinoam Sapir says that "never" used as part of an answer cannot be assumed to be deceitful if the question includes "ever." This is because once the interviewer includes "ever" in his question, he primes the suspect to reflect the language back. As with body language, one signal, or word, doesn't tell an entire story, but it can certainly help guide us to our next question.

What about the statement, "That bitch had it in for me ever since I dumped her for her sister"? "That," as we discussed in the previous chapter, is a distancing term used by the speaker to create space or separation from the subject, person, or object he wants to avoid association with. The opposite word would be "this," which indicates closeness—or a felt connection. In this example, the boyfriend sets distance between himself and his last girlfriend, who apparently didn't understand his need to date her entire female family line.

Fake your understanding by agreeing with him. Say it would be hard "not to hit" someone who causes so much aggravation. He hasn't recognized it for what it could mean to him, but you have just admitted a propensity toward violence yourself—just for different reasons, as he will soon find out.

Watch for a nod of agreement, and if it happens, jump on it. "Did she push you to the point that all you could do was make her see she was driving you crazy?" Notice there's no blame here, yet. This is just one guy verbalizing an understanding about how hard it is to be a "real" man in this world of frustrating women.

If he confesses everything, be it violence or some other crime against women, be sure that you are close enough to be able to put a hand on his shoulder, but resist the urge to begin squeezing. Keep nodding as he lets it all out. When you've heard enough, let him in on a secret of your own. Tell him you, too, are prone to violent outbursts. Given your proximity, you could go with a quiet, understated whisper when you begin sharing, or you could use a little more volume than necessary, and get his adrenaline pumping. It's up to you. Use whichever you think will have the most impact.

I favor a quiet approach, as it forces the listener to concentrate on the words being said. If you speak too loudly, he may be afraid you're about to become violent, and focus on this instead of actually listening. You have to check the laws in your state, but most states frown upon beating the crap out of egotistical boyfriends. Also, increasing your volume too early will weaken the impact of this form of psychological pressure if you use it again down the road.

The Latin proverb *Timor mortis morte pejor* comes to mind. It means, "The fear of death is worse than death." This could be our motto. With the boyfriend, we want our words and demeanor to imply we are capable of great violence, without us having to showcase these talents. It's more challenging to suggest a potential for violence without actually threatening him than you might think. Of course, if he has admitted that he hits girls, you might find it difficult to remain calm and not slip a rear naked choke on his ass. If this urge overtakes you, be sure to whisper in his ear as he slips unconscious that you harbor cannibalistic proclivities and haven't stocked your basement freezer in weeks. I jest, of course!

If you know he thinks a violent outburst from you is a real possibility, go with it. His own imagination is a good tool to leverage against him. It's far better than you colorfully outlining what you will do to him if he hurts your daughter. At the end of the day, if you've discovered that he feels inclined to hit girls, he should not go out with your daughter at all. Your new goal isn't to try to make him tow the line while he's dating her—your goal is to put him off wasting all of your respective time dating her at all. He needs to know that your daughter is not in the greener, easier field, and that more readily available victims exist. This is not the time to be ambiguous or choosy with your words. You need a statement to indicate what you might be thinking, and let his imagination fill in the blanks.

"You hit your girlfriend because she made you feel frustrated, correct?" To ensure you still have his attention and that he isn't tuning you out, ask short yes-or-no questions and wait for the correct response before moving on. Yes-or-no responses at this time are a must. We want him listening, not thinking.

From here, you can continue with "I move straight past frustrated when I hear about a male striking a female. I jump immediately to rage. Have you ever felt rage?" Wait for acknowledgment, and then go on: "What do you think a father would think it's okay to do to someone who hit his little girl?" A father reference here generalizes the situation, so it doesn't specifically focus on you, but the remainder of the question engages his imagination about what might happen to him if he doesn't do as you ask. He may shrug and play dumb here because he is reluctant to answer. He will know he is being asked to describe a suitable punishment for the crime, and most guilty people don't like to do that. In criminal cases where the suspect is asked by police to describe what punishment he deems suitable for the crime he's being questioned about, the person often includes some sort of leniency or therapy to help the perpetrator "mend" his issues. If he's guilty, he's unlikely to say, "Fry the bastard responsible," because he knows he's suggesting a punishment for himself. Innocent people have little to no problem declaring what should happen to someone guilty of the crime.

So if the target of your wrath suddenly becomes mute, or proclaims that someone like him should be "therapized" back to health, don't let him off the hook. He will probably be squirming at this point, and you will want to encourage him to explain himself. Your goal is to make him so uncomfortable that he never wants to return to your home or get close to your daughter again.

If you still hold a spatial position near him, or better yet, are inside his personal space, ensure that you maintain it while simultaneously blocking the nearest exit. Cops sometimes use this technique to apply additional, but subtle, pressure to suspects who might be on the edge of confession, but need an extra push to send them over the edge. Blocking the escape route when someone already feels crowded and claustrophobic is a lovely way to add pressure.

You could add, "I don't believe in therapy for offenders like this. Someone who hits women should be made to face someone larger than himself, so he understands what it is like to feel helpless and victimized—to be at the mercy of someone who could hurt him a lot." To this, he might not say a darn thing, and if this is the case and all you have managed to do is get him wide-eyed and fearful, then that will have to do. Let him have some quiet moments and don't be in a rush to fill the quiet. Remember the power of silence. Give him time to ruminate on the consequences of his behavior before filling the void.

After you've let the void stretch for what will feel like an eternity to him, break the news: "I know you and my daughter are not a good fit. She is much too opinionated and strong-willed to put up with your sort of behavior. She would never allow herself to be hit. I will not allow her to be hit without there being severe consequences for the striker. Do you understand what I am saying?" Ensure his understanding by insisting he do more than stand there mute.

Once he has agreed to your reasoning and nodded affirmation, it's time to make the final move. Your daughter must come and hear the reasons why this relationship isn't going to work, and she must hear it from him. The two of you should have an understanding that if at any time during your interview he reveals behavior that is dangerous or antisocial, you both agree that this isn't a relationship that is worth pursuing.

Making Junior explain why he knows their relationship isn't going to work eliminates him putting a twist on what happened in the kitchen at a later date. Your daughter will see that you didn't stick his hand down the disposal and make him falsely confess, and he will know she has seen him for who he truly is. Admitting to her that he hits women should be more than enough to eradicate any attraction she might have had for him. In Gavin de Becker's book *The Gift of Fear*, he refers to women who are hit as "victims the first time, and volunteers the second." If your daughter knows her self-worth and understands that a guy who strikes a woman is a coward of epic proportions, then she will have no problem ruling a romance with this piece of work off her wish list.

Once the explanation has been given, ensure that your daughter explains she now has no interest in dating him and that he is to stay well away from her in the future. There isn't any reason for her to expand and threaten him with an ass-kicking from you if he doesn't heed her warning. His humiliation should be more than sufficient to kill the desire on his part, and threatening him with specifics might serve only to undermine what his imagination has already provided in the form of consequences. Additional humiliation could be counterproductive. You don't need to push the message so hard that you send him over the edge and he wants some sort of payback.

Let's take a moment now to recount things we've discussed: If you interrogate the right way, always providing him with a way to admit previous crimes, then he might tell you things you never expected to hear. This is why it's so important to be mentally flexible, ask single and not compound questions, and let his demeanor and answers guide your additional inquiries. You should never presume to know what he might want to share with you. It might be huge in his mind, but small in real-world terms. Ask questions if you are unsure of the intention of the words. His internal dictionary might differ greatly from yours, and you might be alarmed by something he says, only to discover his understanding of a particular term is vastly different than yours. With a little digging, you might discover that he's just a bit of a nervous nelly and his "crime" isn't so bad.

But what if he is too smooth? What if he gives you nothing and seems to be completely at ease during his Q&A time with you? In this situation, it is his lack of emotional reactions that should start ringing your alarm bells. No guy is above feeling at least slightly intimidated by his girlfriend's father, unless the following reasons apply:

1. He really doesn't care about your daughter, and you are a mere bump in the road in his journey to the next notch on his belt.
2. He lacks real emotions, like fear, anxiety, and empathy. Even love is a foreign concept to him.
3. You don't have enough manliness to instill fear in a third grader, let alone your daughter's jock boyfriend, so you, my friend, will need to up your man-game.
4. He really doesn't have anything to hide.

Whether he sets your teeth on edge or not, if you have interviewed him well and he hasn't given you a reason to pull the plug on the date, then it's time to address the eight-hundred-pound gorilla in the room, sex. This conversation couldn't be more uncomfortable for either of you, or be a topic that a dad and boyfriend would want to talk about less. This is why you should be the one to bring it up.

Making him think that you and your daughter have no topic that is off-limits might make him want to play it safe by abstaining. Now that we've got that joke out of the way, the next best goals are safety and preplanning. I, for one, would rather hit my fingers with a hammer than think about engaging in conversations about sex with my daughters and their future boyfriends. But if I don't have the courage to be open and talk things through before stuff happens (and use that courage to my advantage), I certainly can't hope that my daughters' boyfriends will do it.

Junior should know that the only one not up to speed on your family's approach to your daughter's sex life (up until this point) is the person with an itch in his pants that is hard to scratch any other way. When teenage boys get worked up, their brains cease to be part of the equation. It is our jobs, as dads, to keep the four brain cells the boyfriend has at his disposal aware of the right way to act, even if his body tells him otherwise.

This conversation is one of the rare occasions when honestly sharing your personal history can aid your point. There is no way you are old enough yet to have forgotten what it felt like to be a young man in your teens with enough testosterone pumping through your veins to kill a small horse. I'm sure consequential thinking wasn't featured too highly in any facet of your everyday life at the time—the same way it's not featured highly in Junior's universe. He is trapped in a no-man's-land of brainless urges, and although he may not know it yet, he will appreciate your maturity and understanding if you bring up aspects of those desires—not the least of which is that if they are below legal age, *then it's illegal.* This point in the conversation is a good time to mention how many friends you have in the legal profession, and if it happens that you donated heavily to the district attorney's run for office, then all the better.

Another approach to the topic could be you bringing up his long-term career goals. This is something that may have been covered during the initial Q&A period, and if so, can be referred back to now. It's a slightly obscure way to bring up the subject of sex, but the shock value will be priceless. It might sound something like this: "Do you recall telling me about your aspirations to be a fighter pilot in the US Marine Corps? You do? Good. Because if you have sex with my underage daughter tonight, or any night before she is of legal age, you are going to need to join the French Foreign Legion in order to escape my wrath. I'm pretty sure they don't have a fighter pilot school, so you'll end up in the camel pilot program while you apprendre parler Français." You should then smile the sort of smile that serial killers use, and watch him go from shock and awe to wither and wilt. Nothing sobers up young passion quicker than realizing Dad knows the game, and isn't afraid to talk things through with you.

I guarantee that this will go a lot smoother if your daughter isn't standing beside him when you bring it up. This is one of the few times that not discussing your tactic with her beforehand is a better play than bringing it up while she is there with him. You don't want her to think that you don't trust her decision-making abilities. You also don't want her to rebel against you. This is a simple man-to-man chat before he leaves with your angel. After they've gone, you have to resign yourself to trusting that the impact of your conversation with him or previous conversations you had with your daughter will keep them smart and steadfast. But saying a prayer won't hurt....

Another direct, and more intimidating, approach if your daughter is underage expands upon the "let his imagination do the work for you" theme. You ask him to explain what he thinks statutory rape means. If he answers that he has "no idea," then he's full of crap.

We all have theories on things, even if we know very little about them. Your question didn't ask him to relay the law verbatim, merely to either share what he does know about it or engage his imagination and take a guess. During police questioning, thieves will often deny having any idea how the item(s) could have been stolen. The last thing they want to do is provide a potential clue or motivation for the theft to law enforcement. A better response for them would be to pretend they don't have any idea about how things could have been done, or even why. Junior will probably jump to the same hasty response method as the thieves. It isn't that he doesn't really have a clue, more that he doesn't want to air the words aloud and show his understanding of them. That would mean being mature enough to acknowledge how much crap he could be in if he was caught with his hands in the cookie jar. It also is a sobering reminder that he isn't nearly as old as he wants to be at this moment in time, and saying aloud that he's still legally a juvenile brings this stark reality home to roost.

Anything you can do to blast holes in his romantic and probably nasty fantasies about the evening's potential reward will carry weight later on. He will likely have spent most of the preceding few days before arriving at your home to pick up his date daydreaming his way through various scenarios, all of which culminate with him and some sort of happy ending. Our job is to convey the stark reality and reminder that fantasies rarely live up to the mental hype. Your imposing broach of the subject should help ensure any inappropriate mental imagery is shattered before they vacate your home.

If your daughter is of legal age, then the next best thing to mentioning jail time is diaper-changing time. There aren't many young men who daydream of having babies. When they do think about having kids, it's more likely that they picture them at an age when they are older and able to listen intently to Dad's sage advice and teachings. Raising this subject at least insinuates the potential consequences of not using protection. Once again a little shock and awe can go a long way! No one expects Dad to just come out and ask, "What are your plans for protection against pregnancy?" By asking this question right before your daughter comes down to start the date, your words are a sobering reminder that bad things could happen if he hasn't planned ahead. You could add that when you think about your daughter getting married, the last thing you picture is you carrying a shotgun to the happy event. But this doesn't mean you aren't prepared to bring one and ensure he doesn't get lost on his way to the altar.

With a little luck his face will flash surprise, shock, or flat-out fear—a combination of all three would be lovely. But if he flashes some sort of self-assured, "I know more than you do, Dad," smugness, don't miss the chance to let him know that your daughter has the worst memory of anyone you've ever met (whether it's true or not), and that if he thinks he can rely on her being on the pill to prevent such a calamity, then he'd better think again.

We had an unspoken code of conduct in the military, and although it has been many, many years since I served, it often enters my thinking and attitude toward others:

Treat everyone with respect. Be courteous for as long as they are. But always remember you might have to terminate the person before you if he turns out to be the enemy.

Those who haven't served in the military might struggle to understand this mind-set. But consider this: while you are enlisted, you might find yourself working alongside an indigenous person in a foreign land, and that person is your ally until the higher-ups decide he isn't. Then he becomes your enemy. In order to do your job, you must stay ever cognizant of the fact that circumstances can change in an instant, and you will need to follow the instructions of those in command, and do it without hesitation. Seconds could be the difference between life and death for one of you. If it must be someone, better that it's him and not you.

We have discussed the potential for the guy standing in your kitchen to be a bad apple. We have considered that he might have some scary character traits and you are going to masterfully draw these out of him with careful questioning, and attention to his answers. But what if he's beyond odd? What if during your meeting, he decides he's had enough of your clever questions and wants to teach you a lesson? Would you know how to defend yourself? Does your daughter know how to defend herself?

The pressure that he might feel while meeting you for the first time is partly born of the unexpected. You have the upper hand because you will be prepared to ask your questions, read and interpret his answers, and decode their meaning. He has no idea what you might ask. He could start out feeling carefree, thinking he has nothing to hide and that a meeting with you is just another progression in his relationship with his girlfriend. He might not expect you to be different than other fathers he's met, and maybe those meetings went fine. No big deal. But maybe the kid is a ticking time bomb, and the anxiety of the meeting has already put him on edge. One small figurative push from you and he will lose it—potentially violently. Are you prepared if the circumstances change on a dime and he crosses the line?

Violent encounters fall into two categories: premeditated and spontaneous. I doubt that he is going to have spent the afternoon planning and thinking about all the ways he is going to punch your lights out if the introduction doesn't go his way, but I wouldn't rule it out either. Plan for the worse and hope for the best.

If he does have violent inclinations, then your strategy of asking him direct questions and leaping off his responses to provide a framework of follow-up inquiries might be all the ammunition he needs to move into spontaneous outburst mode. If you consider this a possibility, you will be better prepared and much less likely to be caught off guard if it happens.

My childhood makes it easier for me to predict violence than for other people. Most people didn't grow up needing to be watchful of nonverbal indicators of an attack, so they are more likely to not see a bad thing coming until it's too late. This is why so many people who are victims of violent crime tend to profess it "came out of nowhere." Well, unless they were literally ambushed by their attacker, there was likely some indication that things were about to go south. You need to accept that there's a chance an attack might happen, and be on the lookout for indicators of one coming. If you think something like this could never happen to you, then you won't see the warning signs.

At the time of this writing, there is a new craze called the "knockout game." This random act of violence is delivered upon unsuspecting people by a group of youths intent on recording themselves punching some poor person unconscious. This is happening in a multitude of cities, and nearly all of the victims have stated that they didn't see it coming. Well, you can't see what you aren't looking for. The terms for this are "situational blindness" and "normalcy bias." What they mean is that because something like this has never happened to a person before, his or her brain ignores warning signs of danger, and filters out important information with unimportant information.

Realistically, if the boyfriend attacks a big ugly bruiser like you, especially in your own home, you might be able to take him—but your daughter might not be able to do so. Beyond the physical danger, the mental shock she will experience if someone she cares for attacks her could be paralyzing, especially if she isn't mentally prepared.

If the boyfriend has a past history of violence, then the chances that he will be violent again at some point in the future rise considerably. Common indicators of violent intent include glaring of the eyes and/or a lowering of the brows, and lips compressing and/or tightening, which typically makes the lip color dissipate. The person might also draw his lips back to reveal his teeth; he might begin clenching and unclenching his hands; and he might seemingly defy gravity by bouncing on the balls of the feet (if this occurs, attack is likely to immediately follow). Conversely, you may see a sudden drop or decrease in all movements.

Depending on your confidence or skill level as a scrapper, there are a couple ways to comport yourself and defuse the situation before an attack. Most importantly, remain calm. This is easier said than done, but escalating your behavior to match his might be a recipe for disaster. It's especially important in this situation to take full, deep, and measured breaths. Your heart rate is going to be elevated, but full, deep, and measured breaths should prevent it from escalating further, and also keep the pitch of your voice from rising. There's nothing worse than trying to say something in a crisis and discovering that only dogs can hear you. Controlling the rise of your heart rate is also key to thinking as clearly as possible, and maintaining fine motor control.

One of the leading instructors on the effects of stress on the human body and psyche in reaction to violence is Lt. Col. Dave Grossman. He is the author of *On Combat: The Psychology and Physiology of Deadly Conflict in War and in Peace*, a fascinating study on how fear and stress can affect the human body, from brain to toes. When these emotions push the heart rate way up (between 145 and 175 beats per minute), the parts of the brain that make you the calm, collected stud-muffin you are shut down—and other more primitive areas begin taking over. This is why it is so hard to make a solid argument when you're overtaken with anger. Your brain redirects cognition to the parts of it that are responsible for freezing, running, and fighting. Stringing a decent sentence together can become all but impossible.

The less exposure one's had to violence and dangerous situations, or episodes that came close, the more pronounced this reaction can become. This is why soldiers, firefighters, medics, and law enforcement officers train under high-stress scenarios. The scenarios prepare them for the mental and physiological stress they might face while on duty, and condition them to think clearly during it. If it looks like you are about to be attacked in your kitchen by an angry boyfriend, then I'm going to go out on a limb and conclude that you are pretty stressed. You cannot afford to get caught up emotionally in the moment. Stay calm. Lift your hands up, slightly staggered and in line with your chest, palms toward Grumpy. Don't worry, you aren't positioning them like this because you actually intend to surrender. But unless you are Bruce Lee, with reflexes like a cat, keeping your hands by your sides means they have farther to travel if they need to defend you than if they are in front of your chest. If you are going to get your ass kicked, you will want it to be because he has much greater skills than you, not because you left your hands down by your sides and never even gave yourself a chance.

While your hands are up and form a barrier between the two of you, do not tell him to calm down. He may take this to mean that you don't understand why he is mad in the first place—definitely that you think he's overreacting. It is better to make him think that you understand why he's angry and that you want him to talk it out with you.

Depending on the distance between you and Junior at the time of the spontaneous combustion, you might need to be extremely wary. Backing away isn't really an option, as it will make it seem like you're afraid, retreating, or surrendering—none of which are good for maintaining a commanding presence in your home. This is contrarian advice to what I would advise you to do in a public place, which is to create as much distance between you and the attacker as possible. Distance equals time, and time can be a lifesaving luxury in a self-defense situation. But in this case, retreating isn't a good option, as you can't run away and leave him alone and loose in your house.

You are going to have to hold your ground and try to talk him down. This is easier said than done. Nothing about talking someone out of attacking you will be easy, and time is not on your side. It might take him as long as forty-five minutes to find reason and calm down again. You can console yourself during this with the knowledge that your daughter would have an even harder time if he were to level his aggression toward her. You, my friend, just saved her from the violence and duress he could inflict.

With a little luck, you'll be able to use words and a calm, soothing tone to rein him in. But if you can't and he attacks anyway, you had better know how to handle yourself. If he charges and starts swinging at you, bend your legs slightly, cover your head with your arms, and keep one beady eye on him from between your forearms. It is better to see the blows coming and roll with them, than be knocked around left, right, and Chelsea because you've got your eyes closed.

If you are attacked and turtle up, covering your head with your arms and waiting for the onslaught to cease will be the easiest and fastest thing you can do. It can also leave you extremely vulnerable. Just because your head is covered doesn't mean you aren't going to be injured, even knocked unconscious. It is just a fast way to protect your head, your face, and, in particular, your eyes.

On a positive note, most people do not have great stamina. Unless your daughter has brought home a professional UFC fighter, he will likely begin gassing out within a few seconds. Pounding away on someone is much harder than you might think. This is encouraging news for you, as it means the attack will probably be short-lived if you can survive the first five to ten seconds.

Hopefully, he tires out quickly and you can call for the good guys to come and arrest his psychotic ass. Keep in mind, though, that assuming he'll soon run out of steam could be a hell of a gamble. If he happens to have the stamina of a professional racehorse, you might have to change tactics in a hurry.

Being defensive is easier than being offensive, but sometimes you have to fight back. If you don't fight back, things could go from bad to worse. In fighting, there are two approaches: real world and fantasy world. Let me start with the latter first. A fantasy-world approach revolves around the sorts of fighting skills that you see displayed in the movies. They are performed by practitioners with decades of experience and the sort of mastery within each discipline that defies belief. But the tricks you see them use for dramatic effect in movies rarely work in the real world, and they would be the first to tell you so. Then there is the real-world approach. With this, you cannot fight without getting hurt. Even hitting someone in the face with a bare fist often results in extreme physical pain; the fingers can be bent backward, broken, or dislocated.

There are a multitude of martial arts classes that you could enroll in to learn how to fight. I used to teach a combination of Muay Thai kickboxing, boxing, and Commando unarmed tactics. I like boxing and Muay Thai in particular because they are relatively simple styles—and extremely violent, especially Muay Thai. Using a combination of elbows, knees, feet, and hands, you can inflict a great deal of damage on your opponent in a very short time. But I don't think these styles are the best for self-defense. For that, I recommend Krav Maga. This Israeli style of martial art is violent, effective, and as bare-bones as it gets—nothing about the style is pretty. However, Krav Maga takes the best components from a variety of martial arts styles and combines them with some of the most realistic training drills out there.

I know that unless you fall victim to street thugs, the chances of you having to fight are slim, but your daughter might have to. This is why I would like you to take her with you and have you both join a Krav Maga class near you if you can find one. Bonding occurs through shared experiences, and what could be more uplifting and empowering for you both than to attend this sort of class together and support each other through the learning process. The confidence she will develop with these skills will last her a lifetime, as will the memories she forms learning them alongside her dad.

In the Commandos, training was always centered on stress. We were constantly pushed by instructors to stay calm no matter what, and get the job done. If you train in any martial arts skill and the training is void of practicing those skills under real-world stress, then you will most likely crumble and forget everything when the shit hits the fan. You need to practice and train under stress. An old and overused military adage is also true: "The more you bleed in training, the less you'll bleed in combat." One of the principles behind Krav Maga is the importance of practicing under pressure. The real test of any fighting style (and the practitioner) occurs under real-world conditions. Can you perform the techniques when your heart is beating more than 170 beats per minute and your brain has decided to go on temporary holiday?

I was fortunate that over the many years I taught self-defense, I encountered a variety of styles already learned by my students. The styles that I found most challenging to spar against always resided with the folks who had the most real-world experience using them, instead of the more technical, traditional, and clean dojo practitioners. The more precise the martial artist had trained to be, the easier it seemed to pick them apart. If they faced an opponent from their same style, they were great. I'm not saying I didn't get my ass kicked from time to time. But overall, the more inflexible the style, the worse they faired against a style that was adaptable. Krav Maga is practical and direct; it is not designed to be half-assed. It is designed to put the other guy down hard and allow you to escape. If you are fighting for your life in the kitchen, then you cannot afford half-assed Hollywood tricks to stop the onslaught. And if your daughter ever has to defend herself against anyone, you don't want her trying to use something that doesn't work. She must deliver as much damage as possible, and then get the hell out of dodge.

If you two do decide to learn some skills, but Krav Maga isn't taught near you, look for an MMA (Mixed Martial Arts) gym. At least there you will be exposed to a variety of styles including Muay Thai, boxing, and some form of grappling, jujitsu, or judo. Any or all of these would be fine. Sparring will hurt, it's called "conditioning for a fight," but if you want to hold your own in a real-world attack, being conditioned to some pain will help tremendously.

I hit the women I used to train as often as I could (I know how bad this sounds, but it was my job to toughen them up and I did it only in moderation—honest!), and they were always surprised to find out that they were tougher than they expected—and a lot more capable of inflicting damage on someone else than they thought. With some luck, and support from you, your daughter will discover the same, and you two will bond over the experience—magic!

In case joining any kind of martial arts class is not possible, then at least know the areas of the body that are best for you to attack:

1. Eyes, philtrum (right under the nose, above the top lip)
2. Throat (extremely dangerous to strike, but if he's about to stab you with a kitchen knife, then I'd say all bets are off)
3. Celiac plexus (or solar plexus, at the front base of the rib cage and top of the stomach)
4. Kidneys (or anything below the rib cage, front or back)
5. Groin (though men are so wired to protect this area that it can be a tough target to hit)
6. Knees (they do not like to bend from side to side, backward, or otherwise; it hurts, a lot)

7. Front of the shins and tops of the feet (not the most devastating areas to kick or strike, but they will do in a pinch if these are all you can get to)

Notwithstanding all this, knowing how to fight is useless unless you've developed the mental fortitude to do so. This is something that the military refers to as "violence of action." If you are fighting for your life, fight accordingly. Do not go into it thinking, "I'll hit him once and wait to see how he feels about it." Hit him until the threat is dealt with and he realizes the error of his ways. Resign yourself mentally to the fact you might have to do some nasty things to make it stop. In a street (or kitchen) fight, there are no rules. You must do whatever you have to in order to survive. Discuss with your daughter what she should do if she is ever attacked. Then understand that her plan will fall apart as soon as the situation occurs, they always do, and all she'll have left are her wits and adaptability. Improvisation will be the name of the game. Neither you nor she should hold fast to some misguided notion that whatever you thought was going to work will still work if you wait long enough. Think outside the box. Adapt and adapt again if need be. Tell your daughter that in a fight, she is not allowed to give up and stop fighting until she receives written permission from you. Also tell her to hit something on him that is very "soft," hit it hard and fast, and keep hitting it until it stops hitting back. Explain to her that the sooner she dehumanizes him during an assault by mentally referring to him as "it," rather than her date or boyfriend, the quicker she will be able to respond accordingly. If her thought process is, "How could (*Junior's name here*) do this to me?" she will waste valuable time not responding violently enough. If her mind is reporting that "it" is attacking her, she will be better equipped to do what needs to be done to fight him off and escape. Then dial 911 and tell them everything that transpired.

Everything you will ever need to know about the physiological responses to attack, fear, and the gallons of adrenaline pumping through your body can be found in Grossman's *On Combat*. He explains how your fine motor skills will probably disappear in a fight, resulting in you having trouble coordinating your fingers, even to dial 911 after you've put the bugger down for the count. Tunnel vision may also occur, and this is perfectly normal. As is pissing your pants. Once again, the greater your level of training and conditioning, the less likely these things are to occur, but even hardened warriors can experience these responses in a life-or-death situation. If you don't already know this, the aftershock and humiliation post-event can add years to the recovery period. Embarrassment and shame could eat away at you, but there is absolutely no need for that to happen. And however hard this might be for you, it would likely be doubly hard for your daughter, especially if the attack is perpetrated by someone she thought she could trust.

Being attacked in your own kitchen is a worst-case scenario. If for some reason your Q&A does set him off, he's more likely to show himself as an asshole by walking out, rather than taking his frustrations out on you physically. He might call you a few choice names as he retreats, but so what? Your goal is to figure out whether he's a good date for your daughter and whether she will be safer with him or without him.

If he passes your tests with flying colors and seems to have nothing to hide, won't you all feel much better? He'll feel good for passing your interview; you'll confirm that your daughter is the smart, switched-on young lady that you thought she was;

and your daughter will know that if he becomes a permanent fixture in the family, he will be welcomed with open arms—by everyone.

You may have to remind him that nothing extremely good comes easily, and the "never-ending" ten-minute grilling was merely to ensure what your daughter already told you, that he is a great guy. You can tell him that you were just making sure that her high standards were being maintained, and that he truly appreciates his earned place in the family. It might take him a few days, but if he really is a great guy, he'll understand and eventually be glad you did what you did. He will know deep down that someday he is going to do the exact same thing to some other poor schmuck, and guess whom he'll be tracking down for advice? Yep, you, (Grand) Pops. And won't it be a nice feeling to be able to share the joy of how to screen the next generation? Of course it will. You'll love it!

The final part of this book is a bonus chapter added to encourage a conversation between you and your daughter. I've titled it "Just for Her" because it really is for her, but I obviously recommend you read it as well. Believe it or not, her job is even harder than yours. When we become emotionally involved with a subject, it becomes nearly impossible to remain objective. Add attraction to the equation and the fact that she knows he is going to need to be grade-A quality stock to pass muster (hers and yours), and the pressure begins to increase exponentially. She is not a casual bystander, this is her life. The complications that arise from this alone are enough to make finding a great boyfriend extremely challenging.

On top of all this, as she enters her teenage years, she automatically enrolls in the highest risk category for potential victimization. She really has her work cut out for her. The final chapter is a guideline for her to follow that will hopefully cut down her exposure to losers to the smallest figure possible. Life during this period is a delicate balance between alertness, anticipation, preplanning, and backing up her instincts with a tangible checklist to keep her out of danger—all while she enjoys herself as much as she can.

We can't be with our girls all the time. But we can share all the ways we know to help them stay safe, and then love and trust them no matter what might transpire. Your daughter might do everything right, and bad things could still happen. In this case, the love and support of her dad could be the difference between recovery and a deep depression. There must be no blame. You should be a rock of support—a man she can rely on for unconditional love and understanding. If she knows all this before entering this phase of her life, you may have already given her the strength to go against the grain, if necessary, and instead choose to do what's safest. And that might be all she ever needs.

CHAPTER TEN

Just for Her

"Dad should be a daughter's first love and a son's first hero."

—Unknown

Over the course of this book, your dad has gotten to know me pretty well. As this chapter is really for you, I thought I should introduce myself, so you know who the heck is talking to you. My name is Terry Vaughan. I was a British Royal Marine Commando in my early years, a self-defense instructor for many years, and even a competitive shooter on a little television show called *Top Shot*. But the parts of my background and history that will be of most interest to you are what I now do professionally: I am a professional speaker, trainer, and consultant on the topics of reading body language and personal safety. I present to corporate and law enforcement groups across the country, helping them decode and figure people out as quickly as possible. They can then use that information to improve communication, or interrogate a person more effectively—depending on which group I am talking to. My personal safety presentations are particularly close to my heart, as I have two daughters of my own. The information I deliver at these events is the same information I share with my girls.

This book came about in part because after many of the presentations I've given, I would be approached by fathers asking if I had a book that would help them assess and screen their daughters' boyfriends more effectively. At first this might sound like bad news for you—but I'm here to tell you that it isn't, and here's why:

There isn't anything more powerful in a man's life than the first time his baby girl grabs one of his fingers with her whole hand and holds on. The connection between them at that moment will last forever. It is also a catalyst for insanity. I'm not sure exactly when it happens, but there is a moment during that connection when every dad swears that he will never let anyone or anything hurt his princess. He would gladly jump in front of a moving train, or an attacking bear, if that is what is needed to keep her safe. No hesitation, no doubts, no regrets.

It might be hard for you to imagine, but that goofy clown who seems intent on embarrassing you at every opportunity has been thinking about nothing but making you smile, laugh, and feel safe since the day you arrived. There isn't a guidebook for dads any more than there is for moms. We do the best we can based on personal experiences, good and bad, knowing that if we are successful you'll grow into an amazing woman with amazing memories of her childhood. The difference between moms and dads is that mothers will happily call and ask other mothers how they are coping with X, Y, and Z, and what advice they may have to share in regard to the latest challenge of raising children. Dads don't do this. Most conversations between fathers are limited to consoling each other when they find out they will be having a little girl join their brood. They are often teased mercilessly by their mates when the worst among them is rewarded with a daughter. The typical response from the new father sounds a lot like panic, with a pinch of machismo, as he proclaims that his girl will never be exposed to the ills of the world and will be forever sheltered safely in his home. Unfortunately, dads are much too manly to openly share their feelings, concerns, fears, or anything else important with other men. Until they reach a certain age (if then), this just doesn't happen. We aren't smart enough to know what women figured out long ago, that talking things through with trusted friends is the way to make life much easier.

This book has challenged your dad to think about you and dating differently, and even though he would still wrestle a bear on your behalf, asking him to help you find true love is about as scary a proposition as he has ever heard. In fact, if I hadn't written it myself, I might say the idea is crazy. It's certainly a nutty idea for your dad not to defer to the default setting of giving every guy you date a hard time. All we want to do as dads is to shield you from every potential risk to your happiness, and that includes the dangers that come alongside the fun and adventures of dating.

No father wants to lose his position of protector. When the time comes for you to begin making decisions on your own about whom you hang out with, where you go, and for how long, he can no longer provide the sort of security inherent in safely raising you to your current age. As I write this, my own daughters are making grilled-cheese sandwiches, hanging out in their pj's on a lazy Saturday morning at home, safely within arm's reach. It is one of the best feelings in the world, but I know it is going to come to an end. The time is coming when this won't be the case, and I won't be able to control their environment or the people who come into it. They will have to make those decisions for themselves and this is frightening for me, as it is for every dad. But it is natural, and normal. Life changes, develops, grows, expands, shrinks, changes direction, improves, and gets worse, and then starts all over again.

I have tried to provide my girls with the best information and human behavior insight that I can. I want them to make the best decisions possible based on the information available at the time. I also want to be a part of this ongoing process, and I know that if I fall into the typical father role of just giving every guy they bring home a hard time, I will find myself on the "outside" in the coming years, playing a much smaller role than I could have by expanding my horizons. Your dad has decided to do the same, and this is great news for you. Your dad comes to the table with unique personal experiences and perspectives gained from years of life. There is no substitute for those years, especially when they are coupled with a new outlook on how to use them. He still wants to protect you, that will never change, but now, instead of being a potential obstacle to your finding the right guy, he is going to try to help you along your journey, and he is going to need your help to do it.

Don't expect him to turn cartwheels along the way, that might be too much to ask, especially in the beginning. But you can expect him to try to develop rapport with your flame, and ask him some poignant questions when he comes around. He will carefully watch his responses and listen intently to his answers, all to help provide you with a better profile of who the young man really is. If your new beau is a nice guy, he won't have anything to worry about. If he has asshole potential, your dad is going to let you know, and to what degree his deviancy might run. In much the same way as your dad is going to have to trust you to choose your dates wisely, you must also trust that he has your best interests at heart. If he warns you about a particular guy, pay attention. His observations are not motivated by a desire to ruin your dating fun, or to make your life more challenging than it already is. He simply wants to keep you safe and happy.

With that being said, both you and he may do everything right, and you may still end up in danger. You are entering not only the most fun, scary, and happy time of your life, but also the one with the highest exposure to danger. Mitigating that risk is all we can try to do. The greatest tool at your disposal is your instinct. The challenge with listening to your instinct is relying on something without tangible ways to cross-reference why your warning bells are suddenly going off. Unfortunately, we are all more inclined to talk ourselves out of listening to that little voice in our head if we can't substantiate what we feel with logical reasons.

Your friends, who are hell-bent on having a good time no matter what and where it may take them, pose the largest risk of all. We have all had mates who would do nearly anything if they thought it would provide a great story after the fact, or attract a wealth of attention. Whether that attention is good or bad often doesn't enter into the equation. They will look at the other members of the group like they are idiots for not wanting to participate in whatever crazy plan they've hatched, and we, as their friends, are torn between not wanting to look like cowards and not wanting to abandon them when we know it will leave them even more exposed. If you are having this internal conversation, then the toughest thing for you to do is to listen to the inner voice telling you to walk away, but walk away is what you've got to do. Those voices are there for a reason, and that reason is your safety.

It might not be your friends putting you in a tough spot either. Living your life, having a job, and not being a recluse all expose you to some risk—even when you do everything right. I taught a self-defense client who started one of her lessons with me by asking if I could teach her how to kill someone with her bare hands. My first thought was, rut-roh, this could be a major problem. Not many women start learning self-defense with the intent of ending someone's life. More often, they begin because they want more confidence, or an alternate workout to supplement their current fitness regime. Occasionally, a person does it because something bad has happened in the person's past and he or she doesn't want it to happen again; but up until this point, I had never had a woman ask to learn that particular skill set. My first reaction was to say hell no and walk away. It reeked of trouble. The only reason I didn't was because although she at first laughed off the suggestion, I recognized the fear she was trying to mask. I asked her what was going on in her life that she felt this information would help her deal with. She took a deep breath, paused, and then began telling me what was going on. I'll paraphrase here, but this is the conversation I had with her as accurately as I can recall it:

"I have moved apartments five times in the last eighteen months...." In a situation like this, I don't like to interrupt. I want to let the person talk and deliver whatever he or she is comfortable sharing. I nodded and let my sympathy be known through my facial expression. At this point, I didn't know if she was going to be a drama queen making mountains out of molehills, or a bit of a whack job moving wherever "the voices" told her to. This is definitely one of those occasions when I was glad I kept quiet and let her talk.

"I had a great job a year and a half ago and I enjoyed spending time with my coworkers. The only thing I didn't like was where I lived. It was great at first. But after a few months of living there, I started to feel like I was constantly being watched. I would come home from work and things in my apartment would be out of place. Nothing crazy, it wasn't like the place was turned upside down or anything. But I'd rarely wash my dishes before leaving for work and at best I would normally just dump them in the sink. Then I'd come back to the apartment to find them moved. If I had left my coffee cup on the kitchen counter, it would be in the sink. If I put things in the sink, they would be next to the sink. My chair might be moved out or in farther than I remembered leaving it. My shoes from the night before would be on the opposite side of the bed. It wasn't anything bad enough that I knew someone else had done it, especially because it could go for a week or two between these things happening. With that much time in between, I always told myself I must have moved them myself and just forgotten I had. I told my girlfriends what was going on, and they all laughed at me. Some even suggested I must have a ghost. One of them told me to start drinking less, and then these things would magically stop. Only one of my friends was supportive, and she suggested I start taking pictures of where I left things, and then compare the pictures with the placement of things when I returned. I dismissed doing this because it wasn't happening all the time. I decided that it was all my imagination, and I was just adjusting to living alone in a big city. I dismissed it and carried on as if nothing had happened. Then one Saturday afternoon my friends called to invite me out with them, and I started getting ready. I picked out my clothes and laid them on the bed, and I picked out shoes to go with my outfit before hopping in the shower." At this point in her story, she looked as if she was going to cry. I felt bad for her, and I feared where the story was going. She continued, "I finished showering, opened the shower door to get my towel, and all my clothes were laid out on the bathroom floor, right in front of the shower. They were exactly how I had laid them on the bed, except now they were right in front of me!" It was about now that I began to freak out with her. Someone had been in her apartment while she showered.

For months her instincts had been telling her that something wasn't right, and she had done what any normal person probably would have done in similar circumstances—she ignored them. Nothing was bad enough to make her act differently or go to the expense of changing her locks or installing security cameras. Her friends laughed and called her paranoid, but my client realized something was wrong enough to bring it up with them. She didn't want to accept that her instincts were accurate enough to instill a need for positive action. Life lesson: Your instincts will rarely be wrong. And even if they are, erring on the side of extra caution is never a bad thing. You can always laugh it off at a later time, once you are safe.

Seeing the clothes in front of her shower was the final straw. She told me she called her brother and asked him to come and help her move. I thought it was interesting that she didn't call her dad, too, or even the police, and asked her as much. "I haven't spoken with my dad in years, and I didn't think it was serious enough to call the cops." *Not serious enough?* If this wasn't serious enough to call the police, then how bad do things have to be before it is? You don't have to dial 911 unless your life is in danger, but all law enforcement agencies have nonemergency numbers. If you are worried about ending up with some male cop without an empathetic bone in his body, ask for a female officer. She's more likely to understand what you might be going through. With that said, I know a bunch of male cops who would be extremely empathetic and like nothing more than to help a woman in fear.

She told me her brother arrived within a couple of hours since he didn't live too far away, and stayed with her until she was able to find somewhere else to live. She had to forgo her security deposit on the apartment and pay for a couple more months of rent, as she had a six-month lease agreement. None of this mattered. She was so scared at this point that no amount of money lost could stop her from running away from what had happened.

She and her brother hired a private detective to figure out who was behind this. Although she didn't explain how they discovered who was responsible for this creepy behavior, it turned out to be a guy from where she worked. She had never dealt with him one-on-one. In fact, she hardly recalled speaking to him at all beyond a courtesy greeting once or twice. But he had taken a liking to her and that attraction had turned into infatuation.

The fear she had from the experience made her move many times. She left her job, her apartment, and her friends. But the fear didn't disappear. She knew of at least one other occasion when he managed to track her down at her new location because she saw him while she was out shopping one day. Every time her instincts started telling her he was around, she'd move again. She had been in a new apartment for only a few weeks when she saw my flyer advertising self-defense. She opted to try it only because one of the girls at the leasing office told her I was a normal bloke with great skills (her words, not mine). I think she had reached the point that she didn't trust any man not to be a potential stalker, and the referral from another woman helped her make up her mind to learn defense skills—even if they were taught by a guy. I have never felt I was particularly normal, but I did appreciate the sentiments.

My reason for sharing this poor woman's experience with you isn't to scare the life out of you and promote a mentality of "stranger danger" everywhere you go. Her experience was very, very rare. I want you to take heed of the fact that she knew deep down that something wasn't right, but she kept talking herself out of doing something about it. She ignored her gut because her fears seemed unfounded. Most people feel that unless they are facing an axe-wielding maniac, they would rather not admit that their gut has been telling them they're about to be attacked. They would rather not admit to being vulnerable because it offends their sense of right and wrong. We all like to think that we live in a safe society where bad things don't happen. But bad things happen everywhere. One of my favorite things people tell me is, "I live in a nice neighborhood where those things don't happen." This is true—until they do.

The scary example aside, women are much more likely to date a psycho than be attacked by someone they don't know and have had no dealings with in the past. Obviously, you will do your best to screen out the losers and oddballs. Some of them will have such strange personality quirks and egotistical behavior that choosing not to get involved with them will be easy. Still, we are more likely to invite the "bad" people into our lives, rather than become the target of someone we don't know.

But what happens when the individual who has caught your eye turns out to be a bad apple? How hard might it be for you to wrap your mind around the fact that you have chosen a control freak and a person with violent tendencies? No one wants to think they have been duped. But the riskiest personality types are more likely to blind you with their charm and attention because they are so well practiced in deceit and subterfuge. They are masters of manipulation and already understand that if they want to date, they are going to need to act like someone who is likable.

Let's talk now about forming a road map of warning signs that a guy is a nightmare waiting to happen. The best indicator of potential danger and violence down the road is a history of violence in his past. If he's already been in trouble with the law, or is constantly on the fringe of doing so, then one of the red flags is already waving in front of you. Bad boys may have their appeal, but most women go into a relationship with a bad boy thinking they are going to be able to change certain aspects of his personality. Initially, they focus their attention on the nice parts of his persona, "the side of him only they get to see," and they hope to transform the parts of his character they don't like into something more positive.

His routine will begin with massive amounts of attention, charm, and, above all, flattery. When he talks to you, it will be as if you are the only girl in the world; and at this very moment as far as he is concerned, you are. He knows how hard it is to see past ego stroking and excessive compliments because he reacts to these things the same way. If you are a confident girl, with a good sense of humor, then too much flattery is going to make you suspicious. You may know that you are good-looking and a bit of a catch. But if the new guy lays it on with a trowel, he's up to something and it's probably not good. He's hoping that by blowing sunshine your way, you'll eventually wear down and agree to go out with him. Being pursued by an admirer can be flattering. Tenacity on the part of a guy is generally acceptable, if not expected. If a guy wants to date a particular girl, he must show his commitment and feelings for her with attention and enthusiasm. Your instincts and observing the warning signs will need to be the final word on when things have gone too far.

If you go out to eat, watch how he treats the waitress, or even better, the waiter. If he is the nicest person in the world to you, but rude as crap to the server, this will tell you a lot about the type of person he really is. This sort of behavior indicates that he'll be nice to those he needs something from, but someone whom he deems below him will experience the true him.

Your friends may already know this about him. So when they begin asking you what the hell you are thinking going on a date with this buffoon, pay attention. They aren't criticizing your choice, although that may be how it feels, but instead are pointing out the danger looming ahead. They simply can't help but want to intervene. What would you do in their place? It would be hard to keep your mouth shut, wouldn't it? Imagine if one of your friends began dating someone whom she didn't know very well, but you knew him "all too well," you'd probably be afraid for her—and would want to do everything in your power to help her avoid the impending disaster.

Another strategy during your date, beyond observing how he treats other people, is to poke fun at him. You don't have to be relentless; you don't want to send him home in tears. But making fun of him and seeing if he laughs along and takes it well will test the size of his ego. If he can laugh at himself and not take offense, that's a check mark in his favor. If he does get pissed off, it is a huge check mark against him. Lacking a sense of humor, especially as it relates to himself, indicates poor character and a large ego—two things that can become hugely problematic in a long-term relationship.

Problems between you and your friends will begin if you decide to ignore their warnings and carry on anyway. As your friends realize their words have fallen on deaf ears, they will begin distancing themselves from you. If you try to reach out to them to reconnect with them later, your boyfriend may implement a variety of excuses to prevent it. In the same way that your boyfriend was relentless in his pursuit of you, he will now work just as hard to keep you away from your friends and separate you from people who care about you. This is so he doesn't have to deal with them interfering with his actions when he really begins treating you badly. If you start hearing these sorts of reasons from him to stop your wanting to spend time with family or friends, be afraid, be very afraid:

"I trust you; I just don't trust your friends."

"I don't want you to go out without me. Who will protect you?"

"Why do you want to hang with people who don't like me?"

"Why do you want to hang with people who don't like you?"

"You know they hate me."

"You know you get sad when we aren't with each other."

He will find things to say that tug at your heartstrings, make you feel pity for him, and make you second-guess wanting to spend time with anyone else. It might begin to dawn on you around this time that he never wants to spend time with his old friends either. We both know you are a great-looking gal with an awesome personality, but if he doesn't ever want to spend some time alone with the guys or let you spend time alone with your girlfriends, then this is another warning sign that should make you extremely suspicious.

Your family won't have the same luxury as your friends. They will not distance themselves, and will instead be trapped between wanting to protect you and not wanting to push you away. This will be a tough mixture of opposing interests: protecting you while not alienating you. If you continue to date this guy, you will feel as if the whole world is against the two of you, and particularly against you. This has been a part of his plan all along. Step one was to secure a date and win you over. Step two was to begin isolating you. Step three will be to use threats to keep you two together.

The threats may be directed toward you, others, or himself. Of course, if he sees you talking with another guy, then he may not threaten at all. He may just attack. If he thinks he can kick the crap out of the poor guy caught in the middle, then he will. If this is in doubt, he may just take it all out on you later. Jealousy and control tend to go hand in hand with a guy like this.

The self-directed threats may take on a tone of, "If you ever leave me, I'd ____________." You can fill in the blank. He might threaten to hurt your pets, burn down your home, burn down your parents' home, cut himself, cut you, etc. The list is endless, but the motivation is the same: manipulation. He'll gauge your reaction to the proposed violence, attempt to elicit your sympathy, and ultimately begin desensitizing you to various forms of violence (including self-mutilation). If he is able to reference these things and you don't run away, he knows that the hook is being set deeper and deeper. He also knows that the distance between you and those who may interfere with his long-term plans of girlfriend-domination are growing wider and wider. I want you to know that the behavior we are discussing here is a worst-case scenario. Personality problems come in all shapes and sizes. He may never move on to threats of violence, but difficult behavior of a less serious nature—especially if it is manipulative—can still be hard to live with long-term; and anything that makes you miserable should not be tolerated. As dads, we always fear the worst, which is why we are so protective!

The next step in his plan, if you haven't already run from the threats of violence, will be to begin the actual abuse. It may be small things at first. Maybe he grabs your arms during a heated discussion or he shoves you if you say something he doesn't like. Maybe there's a slap. Whatever it is, I can guarantee you that it is only the beginning. He may apologize immediately, but the apology will come with some sort of caveat that will sound a lot like the action wasn't his fault. He may imply or flat-out state that it was your fault. You drove him to do it with your back talk and arguing, and by the time he finishes jibber-jabbering away in your ear, you may well believe him. He will use your own empathy and guilt against you. You may feel pity for him and he will use this as leverage. He may tell you that he did it only because he loves you too much, that he cares for you so deeply that you drive him crazy. He'll say whatever he thinks sounds best and most distances himself from having to take responsibility for the action. If you don't leave the relationship, the cycle will continue to worsen.

He may go out of his way to be especially nice to you after one of these episodes. He will want you to be reminded what a nice and attentive guy he can be when the urge takes him, and he will know that leaving him while he is in one of his nice cycles will be extremely difficult. You will probably think to yourself, "How could I leave him now? He loves me so much.

He has obviously changed, and that bad-tempered flash really wasn't that bad—it was probably just a fluke. It was a one-off detour from the warm, caring person he is, and it occurred only because I inadvertently pushed all of his buttons." You might find a multitude of reasons to explain away his behavior, because you have invested so much time, effort, and emotion into making him a better person.

He will be unwilling to give you up for the same reasons. He has also invested a great deal of time and devotion, only his was into isolating you and making you feel dependent on him. Even if he exhibits this behavior and then apologizes, it is only a matter of time before the cycle begins again. Often this might coincide with alcohol or drug use. If this is the case, neither of these things are the cause of his behavior—they are the excuse. They are merely the facade he is hiding his rage behind. As things deteriorate further, you will know that you have to leave, but if you do, then he will probably do something completely crazy. You know that someone will get hurt, you or someone who tries to helps you.

At this point, you may feel that you can't go home to your parents again, at least not without putting yourself or others at risk, and you may feel that you have to find a way to deal with all this alone. There will be feelings of humiliation and embarrassment, in addition to extreme fear and anxiety. These fears are well founded. It may be at this point that you can't take anymore, and you leave him despite the potential danger. This is when you are most at risk for extreme violent behavior. Beyond anything that has occurred before, his rage in losing control of you will send him to new levels. You may even think (and possibly with very good reason!) that if you report this to the police and secure a restraining order, he's likely to try to kill you. His attitude will be, "If I can't have you, then no one can." Or he may threaten to kill your family. It is at this point that you will feel about as helpless as a person can feel, and even going home may seem an impossible option.

What you need to realize is that your family will not care what motivated your return, only that you have come back!

This cycle of events may sound far-fetched and extreme, but during the years I was teaching self-defense, I heard a multitude of dating scenarios just like the one I've described here. Even now, when I deliver personal safety presentations to women across the country, I hear one account after another of circumstances like this, and sometimes worse. One thing each of the women expresses is that she wishes she had listened to her instincts, or those of family and friends, back when it all began—family, in particular. Knowing and understanding this pattern of behavior in a potential date or boyfriend is incredibly powerful. If you already know what to look for, you are much more likely to recognize the signals well before things reach a point where you think you can't escape.

Dads around the world have a bad reputation for not playing a positive, active role when their daughters begin dating. We don't want to admit you've grown up, and your dating is proof positive this has happened. We all want our little girls to stay little girls! You have been our little princesses since we first held you in our arms, and for those dads manly enough to admit it, we felt like crying for joy when it happened. It was this impact that made us swear to protect you from everything we can, and God help the person who may hurt you.

Then you began growing up. You developed opinions of your own and sometimes they differed from ours. This was a shock! You still laughed at our goofy jokes, but now the laughter was more polite and less rib-crackingly genuine. You began realizing that you were going to need another hero to fill in for your "out-of-touch dad," and your dad probably realized the same thing. Suddenly you are thinking about boys, dating, partying, and other things that completely freak dads out. And because of this, Dad may begin to withdraw. He may talk with you less and less because he doesn't have a clue how to talk with you about things that interest you.

He probably would never admit this, especially to you, but he is scared. He'd still jump in and fight to the death for you, but he isn't sure what to make of your newfound independence. You can help guide him through this. Ask him to promise you that he will play a positive role in this part of your life, as he has done during your earlier years. He will have an impossible time not listening to you if you open the door to this area of your life. You are going to need to be very brave, as is he. Talking about relationships, dating, and, yes, sex is not going to be easy for either of you, especially if you have never discussed any of this before. But neither of you can afford for any topic to be off-limits. You can't dance around the elephant in the room forever, and any topic that creates an uncomfortable silence could eventually drive a wedge between you. Life is too short for wedges… and I don't mean the footwear! As Sophie, my middle child, is so fond of telling me, "There's always time to talk about great shoes!"

As difficult as it will be for me to talk to my daughters about dating and their boyfriends, I would much rather open up the floor to the topic than pretend it isn't happening and potentially lose my close bond with my girls during those years.

You will face some monumental challenges in screening boys for a "winner," and this task is made all the harder when you find yourself attracted to someone who requires careful screening. It will always be in your best interest to avoid entanglements with the wrong guy, rather than having to extricate yourself from a bad apple further down the line. Reading someone and figuring out which category he might fall into is hard enough. What he says, how he says it, what his body language reveals, what makes sense and what doesn't, his tone of voice, gestures, facial expressions, past history is all challenging enough. If you add into the equation that you will also be concerned with whether he likes you, and thinks you are smart enough, funny enough, pretty enough, and all of the "enoughs" to snag this handsome devil, then you will soon find yourself immersed in a situation where your brain is on overload.

Wouldn't it be nice to be able to trust a second opinion, especially if that someone has only your best interests at heart?

The trick is to know that the opinion is unbiased. Your mother might back you up. After all, she's also been there, and so may already feel some sympathy to your plight when it comes to finding a great date. She will also know that you are swimming against the tide when it comes to your dad "approving" any boy for you. His attitude of "no guy will ever be good enough" will most likely never change. But if you can trust him to keep that to himself and have him play a supportive role during your dating years, then you will receive a second opinion from someone who loves you more than life itself.

The two of you cannot arrive at this without having a heart-to-heart and talking first. You may already know this, but we dads are not exactly famous for opening up and freely discussing our fears or feelings. His willingness to read this book and at least entertain a shift in approach to meeting your dates with a positive mind-set is a great sign. It shows that with the right coaching from you, you may be able to begin trusting him to provide you with support, and his blessing, when you bring home a truly nice guy. That will be his challenge. Your challenge will be to listen and heed his worries and concerns when you bring home a guy who isn't up to snuff. Your dad may see something that you are unable to see because you are too close to things. You need to trust and understand that when he says, "That guy is not right for you," he is saying it for the right reasons and not because he doesn't want you to date. He just doesn't want you to date that guy. And if his reasons are based on tangible people-reading skills, rather than a wild gut feeling, you can feel better about his advice.

The two of you must decide how you intend to handle a situation like this well in advance of it happening. Trying to fumble your way through making the correct call when emotions are involved and everyone has a strong opinion will be a recipe for disaster. The two of you cannot afford a fallout over one of your dating choices. The damage might be irreparable. There should never come a time when you cannot comfortably turn to your dad and say, "I need your help." He must understand that it is his job to be available and not judge you, no matter what decisions led to the need for consolation and support. And you need to know that you always have a place to return to that is safe, loving, and supportive.

There is good news among all of this worry about the dangers we dads think you might face: nearly all of them will never occur. One of the hardest challenges in a young woman's life will be to truly believe in her self-worth. Many of the difficulties you might face through your dating years can be minimized if you know how deserving you are. If you know in your heart that you are worthy of being treated well, then you won't ever settle for anything else. This is something I'm sure your dad will back you up on.

In regard to other matters of safety, with stranger danger being one of them, attention to your surroundings is easy to practice and can pay dividends in lowering your risk exposure. Tuning in to what's going on around you doesn't need to make you paranoid. For the first couple of weeks of really paying attention, you might feel as if you have put your head on a swivel, and that it's a lot of hard work; but like any new habit, once you have practiced for a while, it will become second nature.

When I present my personal safety seminars, I deliver three to seven hours of information, far too much for a condensed piece like this. In lieu of that, I'll share one of the many acronyms the military and intelligence agencies teach their operatives about staying safe. These are the guys constantly in danger, and they are definitely in need of simple guidelines to remind them to be vigilant—just like your father's daughter. Thus, I give you TEDD—Time, Environment, Distance, Demeanor.

Time: Time can be applied to the number of times you might have seen the same individual, the time of day something occurs or catches your eye, and how many times you have habitually been to the same location. Routine is one of the easiest ways for an attacker to reach his target, so be a little unpredictable. Regularly alter things like the amount of time you spend coming and going from places, your routes to and from there, etc., and you will have gone a long way toward making yourself a harder target.

Environment: Your environment can be your friend or your enemy. Always be aware of how many entrances and exits are around you. Never go into a room, building, or restaurant without knowing how to get out using the fastest possible route. My kids and I have played a game since they were old enough to know what an exit is. In it, they count doors into and out of any building we enter. We include all forms of exits, even ones we wouldn't typically use, like staff or kitchen exits; and we take care to note which exits are closest to where we are standing or sitting.

Environment also applies to using cover, versus finding concealment. In an age when active shooters seemingly pop up in every soft-target* facility they can find, understanding that using cover is different than finding a place to hide can be crucial. Cover protects you while concealment merely hides you. Concrete walls at least four inches thick will hold up better than wood. Wheel wells on cars, as well as the engine block, will provide better cover than any other part of a vehicle. If you find yourself in a situation where hiding is your only option, then hide behind something as sturdy and as solid as you can find.

If you have a chance, run as fast as you can, ideally in a zigzag fashion, putting as much distance between you and the shooter as possible. Most people are bad shots under non-stressful circumstances. If they are moving, their target is moving, and if there is some distance between you both, then they probably couldn't hit a barn door, let alone your road-runner swiftness. Increasing that gap as erratically as possible will make things even more difficult for them, and could be a lifesaving maneuver.

---

* A soft target tends to be a location with a high populace of unarmed people who are an easy target to hurt and victimize.

Distance is also important for a couple of other reasons. First, any guy who stands closer to you than you are comfortable with is trying to dominate your space. Personal zones are hugely significant because if you see the same guy not crowding other people, then there is something about you that makes him think he can get all up in your schnizzle. If this isn't where you want him to be, don't be afraid to tell him to back off. It is better to find out now that he's a bad guy than for you to play it safe by being polite and not saying something. Distance is also important because the more of it you have around you, the more time you have to make a decision about where to run to, or what else you might be able to use within your environment to defend yourself. Note, though, that attackers often maintain a safe (nonthreatening) distance between themselves and their targets while they scope them out. They maintain this distance right up until they decide whether to spring an ambush or go find an easier, less-attentive target.

Demeanor is exactly what you might think it is: how you move within your surroundings, or how other people do. Looking up, looking around, and paying attention, rather than being buried reading the latest text from your girlfriend, indicates you are switched on and not prone to space out and ignore what's going on around you. As for other people, when someone is up to no good, they typically limit head and arm movements as a means of attracting less attention. If you ping someone acting odd, this might be what your subconscious or conscious has identified.

If someone looks unnatural in his environment, even if you can't quite identify why, chances are it is something about the person's movement that is wrong. Do not second-guess yourself. You never see a squirrel (or anything else in nature) run away from a threat and then start calling himself names because he feels foolish for thinking he was in danger. You shouldn't either. If it feels wrong, don't worry about what or why—just leave.

If you use TEDD as a guideline in your everyday life, you'll cut down the potential for you to ever be a victim of anything. If you and your dad communicate about your various expectations during your time dating, life will be much easier on both of you! In fact, it will be nice to know that he's not running interference and is actually bringing his many years of experience to bear on your behalf. There isn't a man anywhere in the world who cares more about you being happy, safe, and eventually settled down with a family of your own than your dad. If you both work together toward that end, the two of you will always be close, and also one hell of a formidable team in search of Mr. Right.

Resources

Internet Resources

Dads' Club website: www.tvempowers.com/dads

Paul Ekman's website: www.paulekman.com

Humintell's website: www.humintell.com

Glenna Trout's website: www.itsallaboutface.wordpress.com

Founder of SCAN Avinoam Sapir's website: www.lsiscan.com

Mark McClish's website: www.statementanalysis.com

Peter Hyatt's website: www.statement-analysis.blogspot.com

Books

Confessions of a Sociopath: A Life Spent Hiding in Plain Sight, M. E. Thomas

The Expression of the Emotions in Man and Animals (second edition), Charles Darwin, edited by Joe Cain and Sharon Messenger

Telling Lies: Clues to Deceit in the Marketplace, Politics, and Marriage, Paul Ekman

Unmasking the Face: A Guide to Recognizing Emotions from Facial Expressions, Paul Ekman

Face Reading in Chinese Medicine (second edition), Lillian Bridges

"The Dark Triad of Personality: Narcissism, Machiavellianism, and Psychopathy," *Journal of Research in Personality*, 36 (2002), 556–563, Delroy L. Paulhus and Kevin M. Williams

Narcissism: Behind the Mask, David Thomas

"The Dark Triad: Facilitating a Short-Term Mating Strategy in Men," *European Journal of Personality* Volume 23, Issue 1 (2009), Peter K. Jonason, Norman P. Li, Gregory D. Webster, and David P. Schmitt

The Sociopath Next Door, Martha Stout

Social Psychology (third edition), Robert S. Feldman

10 Easy Ways to Spot a Liar: The Best Techniques of Statement Analysis, Nonverbal Communication, and Handwriting Analysis, Mark McClish

Don't Be Deceived: The Definitive Book on Detecting Deception, Mark McClish

The Gift of Fear and Other Survival Signals That Protect Us from Violence, Gavin de Becker

On Combat: The Psychology and Physiology of Combat in War and in Peace, Dave Grossman and Loren W. Christensen

Acknowledgments

I would like to thank my wife, Carol, and our kids, Cora, Sophie, and Aidan, who asked me every day how my writing went that day, and then listened patiently while I told them every detail. Thanks also to my editor, Julia Abramoff, who bravely stepped up to the plate and made my crazy ambitions a reality—cheers!